NOV 2007

31 x 5/21 -W

J 975.9 ORR
Orr, Tamra.
Florida /
2007/11/19

D0460923

How to Use This Book

Look for these special features in this book:

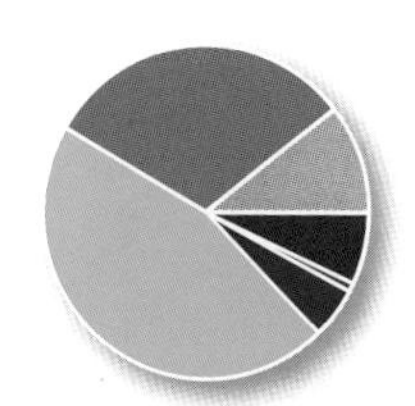

SIDEBARS, **CHARTS**, **GRAPHS**, and original **MAPS** expand your understanding of what's being discussed—and also make useful sources for classroom reports.

FAQs answer common **F**requently **A**sked **Q**uestions about people, places, and things.

WOW FACTORS offer "Who knew?" facts to keep you thinking.

TRAVEL GUIDE gives you tips on exploring the state—either in person or right from your chair!

PROJECT ROOM provides fun ideas for school assignments and incredible research projects. Plus, there's a guide to primary sources—what they are and how to cite them.

Please note: All statistics are as up-to-date as possible at the time of publication.

Consultants: Benjamin D. Brotemarkle, Professor of Humanities,
Brevard Community College; William Loren Katz; Walt Schmidt, Florida State Geologist
and Chief, Florida Geological Survey

Book production by The Design Lab

Library of Congress Cataloging-in-Publication Data
Orr, Tamra.
Florida / by Tamra B. Orr.
p. cm.—(America the beautiful. Third series)
Includes bibliographical references and index.
ISBN-13: 978-0-531-18558-2
ISBN-10: 0-531-18558-3
1. Florida—Juvenile literature. I. Title. II. Series.
F311.3.O77 2008
975.9—dc22 2006100102

No part of this publication may be reproduced in whole or in part, or stored in a retrieval system, or transmitted in any form or by any means, electronic, mechanical, photocopying, recording, or otherwise, without written permission of the publisher. For information regarding permission, write to Scholastic Inc., 557 Broadway, New York, NY 10012.

©2008 Scholastic Inc..
All rights reserved. Published in 2008 by Children's Press, an imprint of Scholastic Inc.
Published simultaneously in Canada. Printed in the United States of America.
SCHOLASTIC, CHILDREN'S PRESS, and associated logos are trademarks and/or registered trademarks of Scholastic Inc.

1 2 3 4 5 6 7 8 9 10 R 17 16 15 14 13 12 11 10 09 08

Florida

BY TAMRA B. ORR

Third Series

Alameda Free Library
1550 Oak Street
Alameda, CA 94501

Children's Press®
A Division of Scholastic Inc.
New York ★ Toronto ★ London ★ Auckland ★ Sydney
Mexico City ★ New Delhi ★ Hong Kong
Danbury, Connecticut

CONTENTS

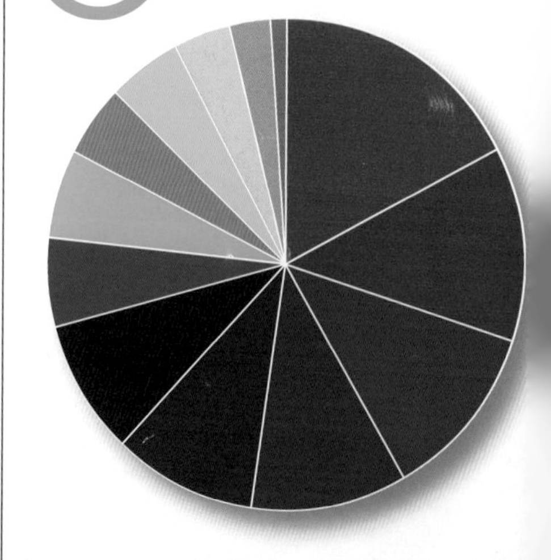

GROWTH AND CHANGE

4
Wars rip through the state, and a new century brings new businesses and the chance to become a millionaire. . . **48**

MORE MODERN TIMES

5
Home to rocket ships, a growing Latino community, and numerous tourist destinations, Florida keeps up with big changes. **58**

TRAVEL GUIDE

9
Check out historic towns, collect seashells at the beach, or visit a world-famous mouse. . . . **104**

PROJECT ROOM

★

PROJECTS. 116
TIMELINE 122
GLOSSARY 125
FAST FACTS 126
BIOGRAPHICAL DICTIONARY. . .133
RESOURCES 137

★

INDEX. 139
AUTHOR'S TIPS AND SOURCE NOTES. 143

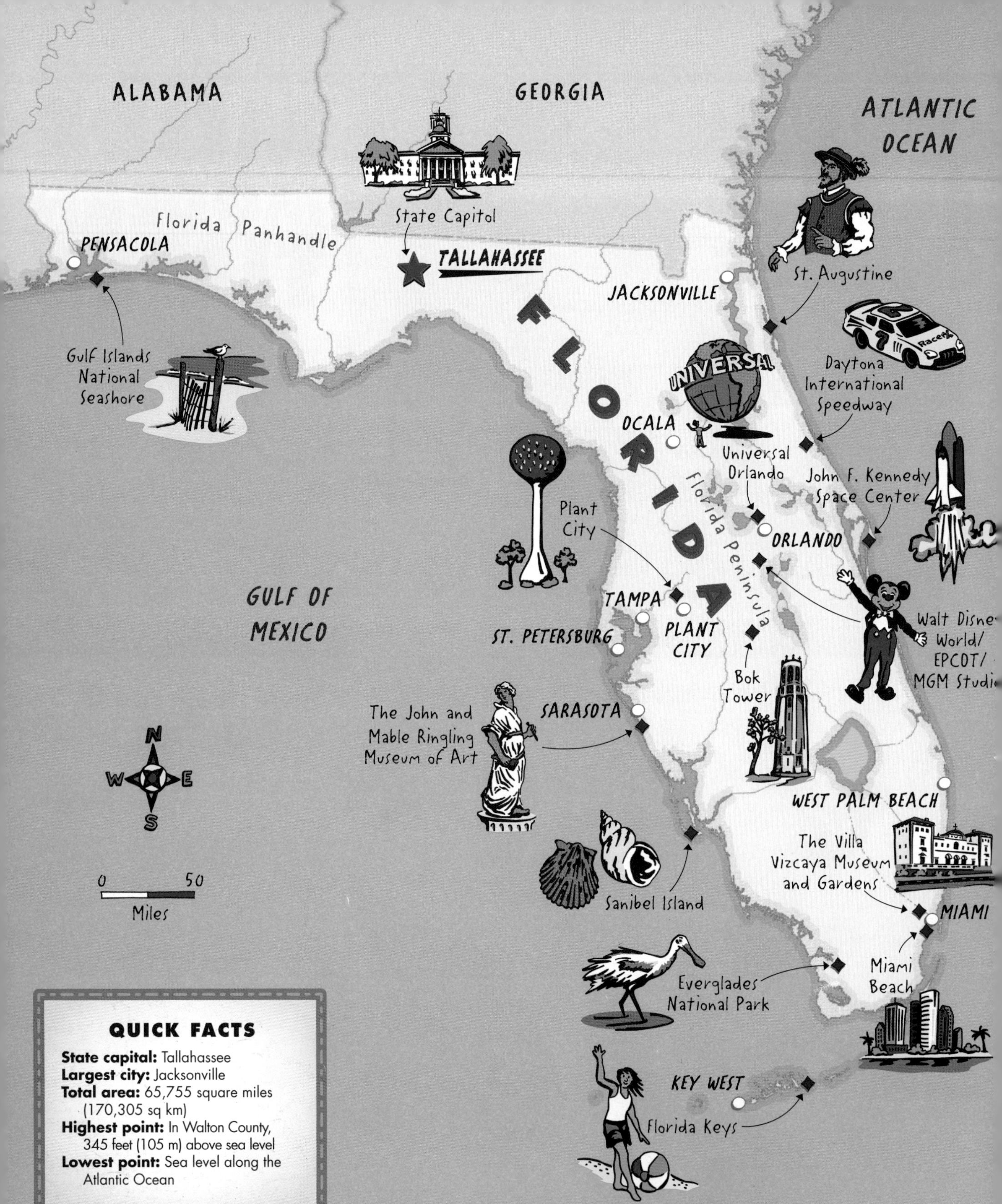

QUICK FACTS

State capital: Tallahassee
Largest city: Jacksonville
Total area: 65,755 square miles (170,305 sq km)
Highest point: In Walton County, 345 feet (105 m) above sea level
Lowest point: Sea level along the Atlantic Ocean

Welcome to Florida!

HOW DID FLORIDA GET ITS NAME?

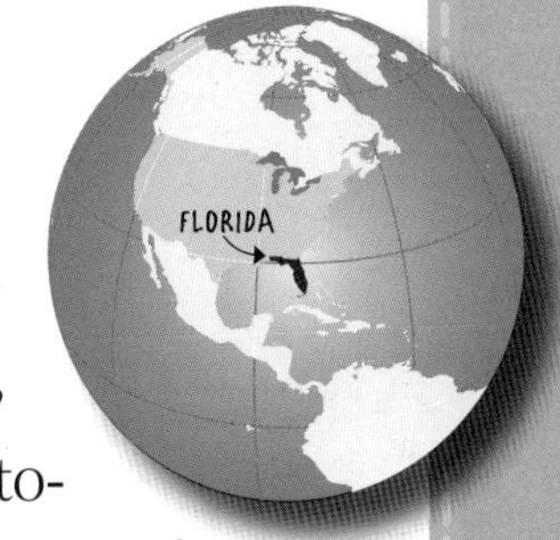

Juan Ponce de León was the first European to come to Florida's shores, almost 500 years ago. Some historians believe the Spaniard arrived in the spring and was so overwhelmed by all of the beautiful and colorful blooming flowers that he named the land *la florida,* which means "the flowery one" in Spanish. Others believe he got there on Easter, so he named it in honor of Pascua Florida, or "the feast of flowers," a festival held on that day in his country. Either way, historians agree that this explorer gave Florida its name!

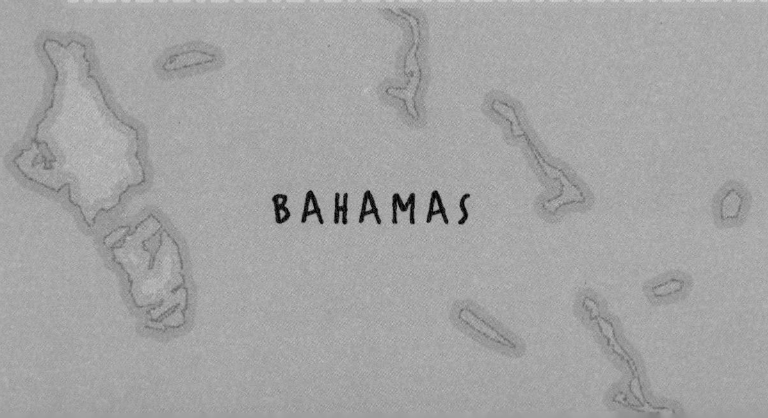

FLORIDA

BAHAMAS

READ ABOUT

The Florida Everglades is home to a variety of birds, including white egrets and ibis.

LAND

★

JUST HEARING ABOUT FLORIDA MAKES MANY PEOPLE THINK OF SUN, SAND, AND SURF. For more than a century, this southern state has been a favorite place to go when cold weather hits the northern states. Its 65,755 square miles (170,305 square kilometers) boast beautiful beaches, rolling hills, and lakes full of wildlife. But don't expect tall mountains. The state's highest point in Walton County is just 345 feet (105 meters). And its lowest point is at sea level along the Atlantic Ocean. But from top to bottom, it is a state brimming with excitement and interesting places.

THE BEGINNING

If you look at Florida on a map, it's probably easy to imagine the state as an island. Indeed, for most of its long history, Florida was underwater. But, because it is attached to the rest of the continent, it is called a **peninsula**. A peninsula is a large mass of land that sticks out into a body of water; in this case, the Atlantic Ocean to the east and the Gulf of Mexico to the west. The body of water between the Atlantic Ocean and the Gulf of Mexico is known as the Straits of Florida. The northern end of the state shares a border with Georgia and Alabama. It is known as the Panhandle because of its unusual shape.

WORD TO KNOW

peninsula *a large mass of land that extends into a body of water*

Here is an aerial view of Florida and the southeastern United States. It's easy to see that the state is a peninsula, with water on three sides.

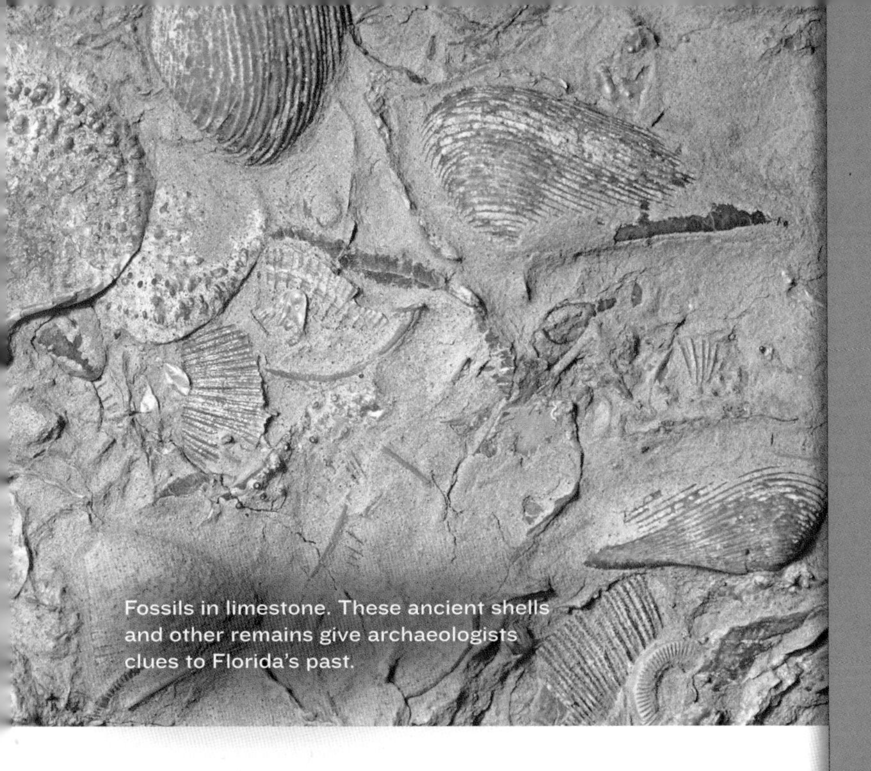
Fossils in limestone. These ancient shells and other remains give archaeologists clues to Florida's past.

WHAT'S IN YOUR YARD?

Do you dream of finding fossils in your backyard? Come to Florida! Here people have found 45-million-year-old sand dollars, not to mention teeth dating back over 10,000 years. Florida's oldest vertebrate fossil, a partial skeleton of an aquatic turtle, was recovered about 50 years ago near Lake Okeechobee. Florida has lots of limestone. It's made out of the shells of ancient animals that once lived in the shallow seas that covered the state. In addition to seashells, occasionally a shark tooth will wash up on the shores, along with bones of different marine animals. Other fossils are found in Florida's caves, rivers, quarries, and mines.

Millions of years ago, multiple giant landmasses, including one called Gondwana, came together to form a single supercontinent called Pangaea. Eventually, Pangaea began dividing into two landmasses, Laurasia (North America, Greenland, Europe, and parts of Asia) and Gondwanaland (South America, Africa, India, Australia, and Antarctica). The area that would later become Florida was in the middle of this big breakup. When Pangaea finally split apart, Gondwanaland was missing a piece of its old self. Laurasia had dragged away the rock material that would eventually become the foundation for the Florida platform.

Florida Geo-Facts

Along with the state's geographical highlights, this chart ranks Florida's land, water, and total area compared to all other states.

Total area; rank	65,755 square miles (170,305 sq km); 22nd
Land; rank	53,927 square miles (139,671 sq km); 26th
Water; rank	11,828 square miles (30,634 sq km); 3rd
Inland water; rank	4,672 square miles (12,100 sq km); 4th
Coastal water; rank	1,311 square miles (3,395 sq km); 6th
Territorial water; rank	5,845 square miles (15,139 sq km); 2nd
Geographic center	In Hernando County, 12 miles (19 km) northwest of Brooksville
Latitude	24° 30′ N to 31° N
Longitude	79° 48′ W to 87° 38′ W
Highest point	In Walton County, 345 feet (105 m)
Lowest point	Sea level along Atlantic Ocean
Largest city	Jacksonville
Longest river	St. Johns River, 275 miles (443 km)

Source: U.S. Census Bureau

Florida is the 22nd-largest state in the country. Rhode Island would fit inside Florida more than 42 times!

Florida Topography

Use the color-coded elevation chart to see on the map Florida's high points (yellow to orange) and low points (green to dark green). Elevation is measured as the distance above or below sea level.

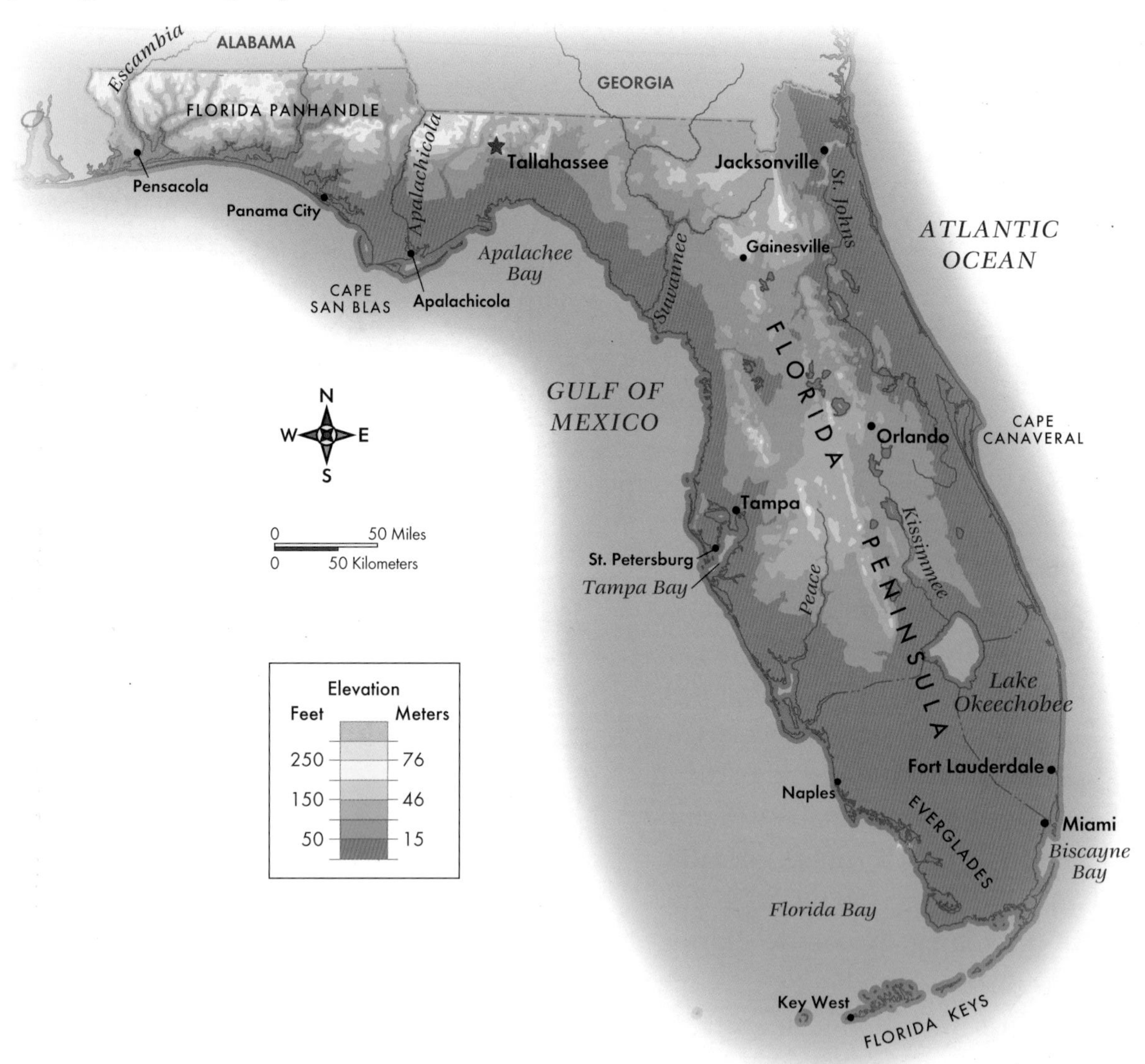

LAND REGIONS

Over time, Florida's topography began to take shape. Geologists divide the landscape into three main regions: the Florida Uplands, the Gulf Coastal Plain, and the Atlantic Coastal Plain.

Lake Okeechobee is the largest lake in Florida. Here, a fishing boat maneuvers its waters, which average only about 8 feet (2.4 m) deep.

The Florida Uplands

The Florida Uplands region divides the Gulf Coastal Plain into two parts. This region runs about 275 miles (443 km) from west to east and then heads south into central Florida. Here are the state's only real hills, which are mostly made out of red clay and sand. The state's highest point is here, just south of the Alabama border. Britton Hill in Walton County is 345 feet (105 m) above sea level. It is the lowest state high point in the whole country!

If you think of the ocean and the gulf when you think of Florida, you might be surprised to know that this region has more than 30,000 lakes in it. Some are only a few inches deep, and some reach depths of 30 feet (9 m). Lake Okeechobee is the largest of them all. It covers 700 square miles (1,813 sq km) in southern Florida but is shallow, averaging only about 8 feet (2.4 m) deep. Florida also has more than 700 springs; some have water-filled caves deeper than 300 feet (91 m).

The Gulf Coastal Plain

This region, which actually appears in two parts of Florida, is found in the west and the northwest. In southwestern Florida, the region extends inland and covers parts of the Big Cypress Swamp and the Everglades. The northern part curves around the upper edge of the Gulf of Mexico and goes west along the Panhandle.

Near Marianna, Florida Caverns State Park allows visitors a glimpse into the history of the state's formation. As water dripped through the porous limestone layer of the land, it dissolved the calcium in the stone. These calcium-filled drops fell to the cavern floor and also clung to the ceiling of the caves. Over tens of thousands of years, they formed into **stalactites** and **stalagmites**. When they grew together in the middle, they made columns. These caves cover more than 10 acres (4 hectares) and were used in the past as hideout spots for Native Americans during the Seminole Wars.

WORDS TO KNOW

stalactites *columns or pillars formed on the roof of a cave from dripping groundwater*

stalagmites *columns or pillars formed on the floor of a cave from dripping groundwater*

Columns have formed from stalagmites and stalactites in the Enchanted Forest Room at Florida Caverns State Park.

This colorful reef is part of the Caribbean Reef off the Florida coast.

The Atlantic Coastal Plain

The Atlantic Coastal Plain is the relatively flat land that stretches all the way from Cape Cod in Massachusetts into the Gulf of Mexico. In Florida, the Atlantic Coastal Plain covers the entire eastern part of the state from north to south. Its shores are low and flat with a lot of sandbars, coral reefs, and barrier islands. In between them are lagoons and grassy wetlands known as marshes.

The coral reefs are lovely and fragile. They are made up of the tiny skeletons of the coral **polyps** that live there. One hit or scrape from a boat anchor or fishing spear is enough to damage them. In fact, such damage can cause a deadly **infection** that spreads throughout the reef, killing off coral that took centuries to build.

WOW

Coral reefs can take thousands of years to grow between 1 and 16 feet (0.3 and 5 m).

WORDS TO KNOW

polyps *nonmoving marine creatures that attach to rocks and coral*

infection *the reproduction of microorganisms within a body, creating illness*

SEE IT HERE!

JOHN PENNEKAMP CORAL REEF STATE PARK

Key Largo is home to the John Pennekamp Coral Reef State Park, which was created in 1963 as the nation's first underwater preserve. This area was also designated as a National Marine Sanctuary in 1975. It is part of the Florida Keys National Marine Sanctuary, a paradise for underwater photographers.

In the south, the Big Cypress Swamp and the Everglades cover miles and miles. The Big Cypress Swamp is made of 720,000 acres (291,000 ha) and is home to a variety of plants and animals. It is essential to the health of the neighboring Everglades, which is a huge wilderness area. The Everglades National Park is vast, covering more than 1.4 million acres (566,600 ha), and it houses a delicate **ecosystem**. The Everglades is generally dark and wet, and often you can hear the sounds of trickling water, the rustling of more than 2,000 kinds of plants, and such animals as huge wading birds, panthers, bobcats, owls, alligators, and crocodiles. The Everglades is particularly known for its saw grass, a spiny, sharp-edged grass that grows in dense stands. Though it isn't pleasant for people to touch, it provides food and shelter for many different birds, reptiles, and amphibians.

WORD TO KNOW

ecosystem *organisms and their environment*

The American crocodile is one of the many animals that make their home in the Everglades.

Some people use airboats to get around the Everglades.

MINI-BIO

MARJORY STONEMAN DOUGLAS: GRANDE DAME OF THE ENVIRONMENT

As a young woman, Marjory Stoneman Douglas (1890–1998) moved from Minneapolis to Miami to work as a writer at her father's newspaper. Douglas was a writer whose passion centered on the world of nature. She was fascinated by the Everglades and wrote a book called *The Everglades: River of Grass*. The book changed people's perception of the Everglades, from that of a useless swamp to an important ecosystem.

Douglas served as editor of the University of Miami Press into her 90s. After she became blind, she dictated her life story. In 1993, she was given the Presidential Medal of Freedom by President Bill Clinton. She lived to be 108.

Want to know more? See www.nps.gov/archive/ever/eco/marjory.htm

In 1947, President Harry Truman dedicated the land as a national park. Today it is considered one of the world's most important natural sites, visited by more than a million tourists a year. One-third of the park is covered in water, so boaters and fishers love to stay awhile. Others climb into a canoe or pull on a backpack and enjoy hiking through the masses of trees and other vegetation.

"The miracle of light pours over the green and brown expanse of sawgrass and of water, shining and slow-moving below, grass and water, that is the meaning and central feature of the Everglades. . . . It is a river of grass."

—Marjory Stoneman Douglas in *The Everglades: River of Grass*

THINK ABOUT IT!

Pythons in the Everglades

In recent years, dozens of Burmese pythons have been caught in the Everglades. These snakes can grow to be 20 feet (6 m) long and weigh as much as 200 pounds (91 kilograms). They are not native to the area, so where did they come from? It seems that people buy the baby 20-inch (51-centimeter) snakes as pets and then don't know how to handle them when they get big. Frustrated owners then release them into the Everglades.

But these big snakes are disturbing the natural order of the environment. Explains park biologist Skip Snow, "We are concerned. They are competing with other animals for food, space, burrows, crevices, and rocks. . . . People pay as low as $20 per hatchling not realizing how big they grow . . . But releasing them in the wild is against the law, it's bad for the animal and for native wildlife. If you no longer want the animal, find an alternative."

Source: www.CNN.com, October 22, 2004

One unique part of the Atlantic Coastal Plain is the Florida Keys. And the "Highway that Goes to Sea" is an engineering wonder that connects these hundreds of **keys** off the southeastern coast of Florida. These little islands begin about 15 miles (24 km) south of Miami, starting with Key Largo, which at 30 miles (48 km) long is the longest. They are actually parts of an ancient coral reef that formed when sea level was lower than it is today. All of the keys are narrow, with Key Largo only 0.5 mile (0.8 km) wide. From Key Largo, the smaller keys extend out over the water in a gentle arc southwest.

WORD TO KNOW

keys *low islands or reefs; the word key comes from the Spanish word* cayo, *which means "little island"*

Originally built as a railway in the early 1910s, the "Highway that Goes to Sea" (officially known as the

The Seven-Mile Bridge, shown here at Pigeon Key, is one of the longest bridges in the world.

Overseas Highway) has 42 leapfrogging arches of concrete and steel. It was rebuilt in the 1930s and has been improved several times since then.

The Seven-Mile Bridge is the gateway to the lower keys and is one of the longest bridges in the world. At the end of the 110-mile (177-km) string of connected islands lies Key West, the southernmost city of the continental United States. It is divided into Old Town (west) and New Town (east) by a road known as White Street. In Old Town, the homes date back more than a century. Many of them are built on stilts 3 feet (0.9 m) or more above the ground. They have tin roofs and often are painted in pink, blue, and other pastel colors. New Town is home to the island's commercial airport and rows of shopping centers.

Weather Report

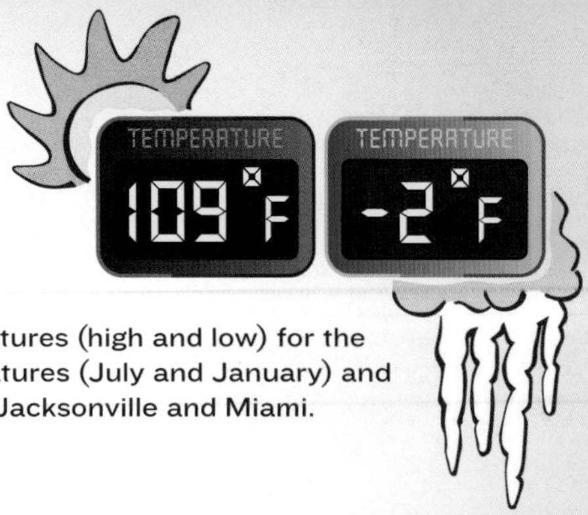

This chart shows record temperatures (high and low) for the state, as well as average temperatures (July and January) and average annual precipitation for Jacksonville and Miami.

Record high temperature at Monticello on June 29, 1931	109°F (44°C)
Record low temperature at Tallahassee on February 13, 1899	–2°F (–19°C)
Average July temperature, Jacksonville	82°F (28°C)
Average January temperature, Jacksonville	53°F (12°C)
Average yearly precipitation, Jacksonville	52.3 inches (132.8 cm)
Average July temperature, Miami	84°F (29°C)
Average January temperature, Miami	69°F (21°C)
Average yearly precipitation, Miami	58.5 inches (148.6 cm)

Source: National Climatic Data Center, NESDIS, NOAA, U.S. Department of Commerce

CLIMATE

One look at the weather report for Florida and it is easy to understand why people call it the Sunshine State. There are warm, sunny days almost all year long.

Florida has long, hot summers that usually reach temperatures in the low 90s at their peak. In the winter, temperatures rarely dip below the 60s during the day, and the state is bathed in sunshine.

In summer Florida's weather changes. Thunderstorms can be hazardous, bringing lots of lightning and rain. Storms become more frequent and intense, often bringing strong winds and heavy rains. Powerful waves, propelled by the winds, crash onto the shore. Late summer and early fall carry the same threat that many coastal states have to face at one time or another: hurricanes. Tropical storms pass through and may turn into full-blown hurricanes.

The total energy released through clouds and rain in the average hurricane is equal to 200 times the electricity the world can produce. Throughout Florida's history, hundreds of people have been killed in these vicious storms, and billions of dollars of property damage have resulted. Floridians had a rough year in 2004, when four hurricanes hit the state. And in the fall of 2005, Hurricane Wilma hit Florida. The storm was responsible for at least 25 hurricane-related deaths in Florida, and it left 3.2 million people without power.

DANGER AT SEA

In 1622, a fleet of ships set sail for Florida from Spain, including the *Nuestra Señora de Atocha* and the *Santa Margarita*. Both were heavily weighed down with cargo. When a hurricane wind blasted across the waves, both ships were sent to the bottom of the ocean—complete with 550 men and treasures.

When Hurricane Wilma swept through in October 2005, wind damage left some property in ruins.

Oranges growing in Lake Wales, Florida

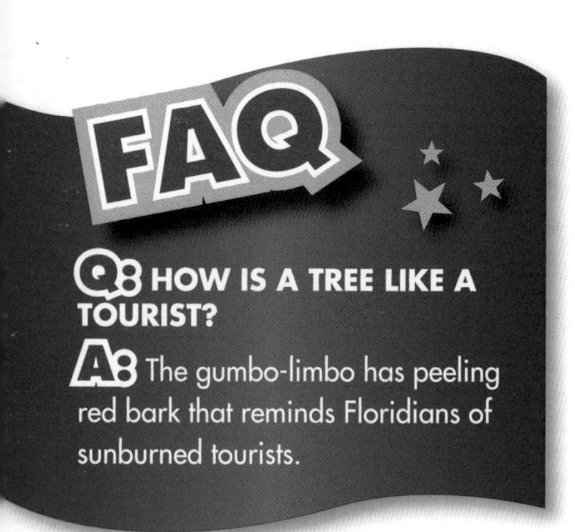

Q8 HOW IS A TREE LIKE A TOURIST?

A8 The gumbo-limbo has peeling red bark that reminds Floridians of sunburned tourists.

PLANT LIFE

Thanks to a lot of sunshine, water, and land, Florida is teeming with plants. Although you may think of palm trees when you think of Florida, only about half of the state has palm trees growing in it. There are actually 11 different kinds of palms growing in Florida, ranging from the royal palm to the cabbage, coconut, queen, jelly, fantail, and Washingtonian.

Other tree species include beech, cypress, magnolia, pine, gumbo-limbo, and mangrove. The mangrove wins the most valuable player award for protecting Florida's environment. Not only are these trees home to many different kinds of sea creatures and birds, but they also help protect Florida's shorelines from wearing away, by acting as a barrier between storm waves and the land.

Many rows of citrus trees dot the Florida landscape. As one of the primary citrus producers in the country, Florida has just the right climate to grow these special trees. Fruits such as grapefruit, oranges, lemons, and limes are tricky to grow because they require almost a year to mature, 300 days of sunshine, and cannot endure freezing temperatures for too long. Citrus orchards are found everywhere, and in recent years have expanded to include more unusual combinations such as tangelos (a tangerine and grapefruit mix), temple oranges (a tangerine and orange mix), and nut-size kumquats.

Because everything grows so well in Florida, sometimes there are plants that are not exactly wanted. The state often has to deal with invasive plants, which can grow very rapidly. They have been brought to the area accidentally through shipping materials or deliberately for landscaping purposes. Since these plants are not native to the area, they don't have natural enemies to keep their growth under control. So they may take over, pushing out other native plant species and limiting food sources for a number of insects, birds, and other wildlife. Groups such as the Florida Exotic Pest Plant Council work hard to increase awareness of this growing threat and to control and manage these unwelcome species.

Florida National Park Areas

This map shows some of Florida's national parks, monuments, preserves, and other areas protected by the National Park Service.

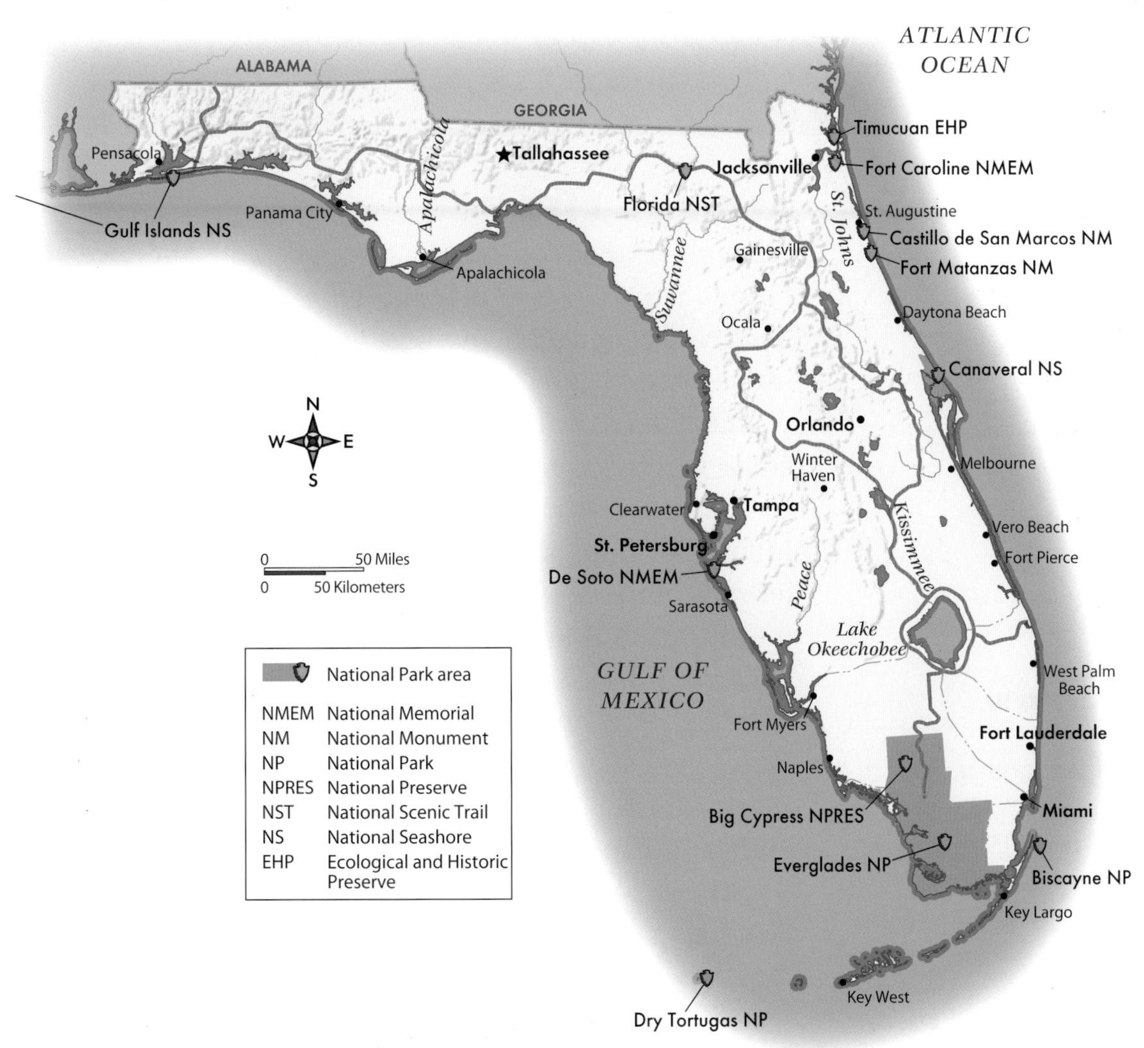

The manatee is a gentle marine creature. A slow-moving animal, it can easily be hurt by boat propellers.

ANIMAL LIFE

With thousands of lakes, swamps, and the ocean, Florida is paradise to fish and other marine creatures. Bass, catfish, bluefish, marlins, red snappers, and sharks thrive here. There are even catfish that walk (called, you guessed it, walking catfish). Shellfish such as clams, crabs, crayfish, and oysters are plentiful, too.

Alligators, known as the keepers of the Everglades, inhabit swamps and rivers. The males often grow to lengths of up to 16 feet (4.8 m), and the females commonly reach 8 to 9 feet (2.4 to 2.7 m). You wouldn't guess it from their dangerous reputation, but these animals help other creatures survive. Alligators dig "gator holes" to lie in, and when they leave, water seeps into the holes. These holes provide **oases** for birds and fish.

The manatee is shaped like a giant potato, with a face like a cute dog and a tail like a beaver. It reaches

WORD TO KNOW

oases *places that provide shelter or relief; the singular is* oasis lengths of 14 feet (4.2 m) and weighs more than 3,000 pounds (1,361 kg). The manatee (also called the sea cow) has lived in Florida for a long time, but is endangered. Slow-moving manatees are vulnerable to encounters with boat propellers—and such accidents account for more than 40 percent of the manatees killed each year. In recent years, Florida officials have worked to educate locals and tourists to be more careful of these gentle, endangered animals.

"Behold the amazing pelican; its beak can hold more than its belly can!" That may be how the old rhyme goes, but it is not quite true. Pelicans do not carry fish around in their pouches. Instead, they dive down and swallow their fish whole. The pouch, beneath the lower portion of the bird's beak, acts more like a fishing net. It can expand to hold as much as 3 gallons (11 liters) of water. These 6- to 9-pound (2.7- to 4-kg) birds have wingspans of up to 8 feet (2.4 m) and can fly as fast as 30 miles an hour (48 kph). On the shores, other waterbirds such as seagulls, herons, and flamingos also look for fish to munch on. The wood stork can be easily spotted by its 5-foot (1.5-m) wingspan. The great white heron is a graceful bird, which can be as tall as 5 feet (1.5 m).

One of the smallest deer in the world—the Key deer—lives in the Florida Keys. There are only about 800 of them, and they range from 24 to 28 inches (61 to 71 cm) tall. Sadly, cars kill about 70 each year. Island officials work to protect this endangered deer by educating natives and tourists to watch out for them.

Other animals found in Florida include black bears, fox, and the Florida panther, which lives in the Everglades. This 6-foot-long (1.8-m), tawny-colored wildcat is endangered, with numbers fewer than 50 today.

A pelican swallowing a fish whole.

IT'S A BIRD! IT'S A FISH!

No, it's actually an anhinga, or snakebird. These unusual birds can swim through the water with only their long, thin necks and heads sticking above the surface. When they see a fish swimming below, they dive and skewer it with their sharp beaks. They come back up and fling the fish off their beaks and into the air. Then, with a flip, they turn around in the water, grab the fish in midair, and gulp it down.

ENDANGERED SPECIES

What do West Indian manatees, Key Largo cotton mice, and Cape Sable seaside sparrows all have in common? They are endangered species in Florida. This means that these kinds of animals are at risk of dying out. But Florida conservationists are working to save these and many other species in the state, including Florida panthers, Key deer, leatherback sea turtles, gray bats, and American crocodiles.

Want to know more? See www.floridaendangeredspeciesnetwork.org

WORDS TO KNOW

jetties *structures that extend into bodies of water to affect the current or protect harbors*

sinkholes *natural depressions in the ground formed by soil, sediment, or rock as underlying rocks are dissolved by groundwater*

International Biosphere Reserve *a protected sample of the world's major ecosystem types*

A Florida panther in a grove of Cypress trees. This animal is one of the state's endangered species.

PROTECTING THE ENVIRONMENT

The people of Florida know what a beautiful state they live in. So they understand how important it is to preserve and protect their natural areas.

Tourists

As you might guess, the number of tourists has an impact on Florida's land. For example, in the mid-1970s, guess what Miami Beach almost ran out of? Sand! Coastal erosion—caused by relentless ocean waves hitting the shore, as well as construction of waterfront houses and **jetties**—made the beaches disappear. Between 1977 and 1981, the U.S. Army Corps of Engineers, in a $51 million beach restoration program, brought in tons of sand to fill up the shore again. They formed a 100-yard wide (91.4-m) stretch of beach for 10 miles (16 km).

Sinkholes

Another issue in Florida is its **sinkholes**. In 1999, Florida's Lake Jackson was just another one of the state's fishing lakes where people liked to spend a lazy afternoon. Suddenly, the lake began to disappear.

Within a few days, the water was gone, as well as the fish and alligators that had been living there. What happened? A sinkhole opened up underneath the lake and all the water drained into it.

Florida has more sinkholes than any other state in the country! Are sinkholes good or bad? Both! Sinkholes are important to Floridians because they create local ecosystems for various animals and plants. Sinkholes provide pathways from which the rain gets to underground water and eventually to people's drinking water supplies. This can lead to groundwater contamination. Sinkholes can also be dangerous because sometimes they open up under houses. In certain areas of Florida, sinkhole insurance is a good idea!

Everglades National Park

The Everglades is the most fragile and the most threatened ecosystem in Florida. Protecting it is important to the state. In fact, the Everglades is not only important to the state, but also to the world as an **International Biosphere Reserve**. Canals and levees built decades ago have diverted some of the life-giving rains that keep the Everglades and the creatures that live there thriving. Pollutants from farming and other businesses contaminate the water. High levels of mercury have been found in everything from the area's fish to its raccoons and now even to the endangered Florida panther.

The National Park Service and the state of Florida have teamed up to try to protect the Everglades before it's gone. Citizens, politicians, public officials, and volunteers are all working together to save this ecosystem through a variety of management programs. With all their efforts, the natural beauty of Florida will be around for years and years to come.

KEY RULES

Florida's commitment to protecting its environment can be seen in this set of rules posted in the Keys:

1. Don't anchor on a reef.
   (Reefs are alive. Alive. A-L-I-V-E.)
2. Don't trash our place.
3. Don't speed.
   (Especially on Big Pine Key where Key deer reside and tar-and-feathering is still practiced.)
4. Don't collect conch.
   (This species is protected.)
5. Don't damage the sea grass.
   (And don't even think about making a skirt out of it.)
6. Don't feed the animals.
   (They'll want to follow you home, and you can't keep them.)
7. Don't touch the coral.
   (After all, you don't even know them.)
8. Don't catch more fish than you can eat.
   (Better yet, let them go. Some of them support schools.)
9. Don't disturb the bird nests.
   (They find it very annoying.)
10. Don't drink and drive. On land or sea.
    (There's absolutely nothing funny about it.)

READ ABOUT

This archaeologist is excavating a Native American burial site on Amelia Island.

▲c. 10,000 BCE
Paleo-Indians live in Florida

5000 BCE
Native Americans form villages along the St. Johns River

▲2500 BCE
Pottery begins to appear, and people spread throughout the state

FIRST PEOPLE

★

IT'S HARD TO IMAGINE TODAY, BUT ONCE UPON A TIME NO ONE HAD EVER SEEN FLORIDA. Nobody even knows exactly when the first person set foot on the peninsula. But stone tools and other artifacts found at Little Salt Springs on the Gulf of Mexico coast of southern Florida date to 12,000 years ago. Many people came from the north, and most settled in the Panhandle area.

200 BCE to 1400 CE
Crystal River area is used as a burial site

▲750 CE
Five Native American tribes are thriving throughout Florida

1500s
First Europeans arrive in Florida

This illustration shows Native Americans on a deer hunt in what is now Florida. Some hunters would wear deerskins as a way to trick the animals.

EARLY CULTURE

Back then, the sea level was lower than it is today, exposing more of the land. Many of the present-day streams, rivers, and lakes of Florida had not yet been formed, making it originally a much drier place. The first residents didn't live in a town or city like your family and friends. They were always on the move, searching for a better area to live. Finding food was everyone's job—including the children's. Girls and women collected fruits, seeds, and roots. Using flint-tipped spears, men and boys spent their days running, hiding, waiting, and hoping to kill a deer or a bobcat. They went fishing for bass, and they hunted turtles to feed their families. The **Paleo**-Indians also dined on animals such as the mastodon and mammoth, now long extinct. With help from their young daughters, the women cooked the harvest and the hunt over a fire pit. The Paleo-Indians searched for water to drink, often digging to find deep springs.

WORD TO KNOW

paleo *ancient, prehistoric*

Since food was plentiful, the ancient people had time to make the other things they needed. Girls turned mastodon bones into sharp needles for stitching sandals. Boys tanned bison hides or sharpened spear points. The Paleo-Indians even made jewelry from bones and seeds. They wove cloth from palm leaves. At night, they slept under bearskin blankets.

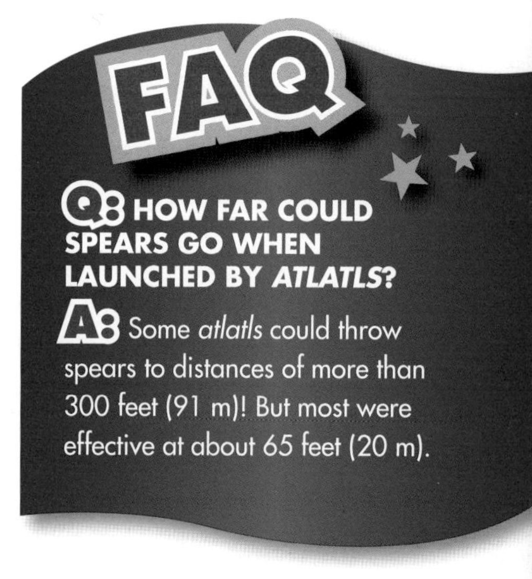

Q8 HOW FAR COULD SPEARS GO WHEN LAUNCHED BY *ATLATLS*?

A8 Some *atlatls* could throw spears to distances of more than 300 feet (91 m)! But most were effective at about 65 feet (20 m).

LIFE ON THE PENINSULA

Over time, the **ice age** ended and glaciers melted. Sea levels began to rise, and Florida started to shrink. Watering holes became easy to find. By 5000 BCE, many of the early people had created villages along the St. Johns River. They developed a spear thrower (called an *atlatl*) to launch their spears at dangerous prey from safer distances. By 2500 BCE, they had begun to make pottery, and people lived almost everywhere throughout the peninsula.

WORD TO KNOW

ice age *a period in history when large parts of Earth were covered in ice; there have been four such periods; the most recent ended about 10,000 years ago*

These are two ceremonial artifacts, one of a deer (left) and one of a pelican, used by the Calusa. They date to as early as 800 CE.

Native American Peoples

(Before European Contact)

This map shows the general area of Native American peoples before European settlers arrived.

The Timucuans of the central and northern regions lived in villages that consisted of individual huts surrounding a larger main building.

FIVE GROUPS PUT DOWN ROOTS

In 750 CE, people on the peninsula began to grow corn. With this regular supply of food, families began to expand and they formed more villages. By then most people belonged to one of five main groups.

Tequestas

The Tequestas settled in huts in the southeast and Everglades regions. They lived on seafood—fish, turtles, snails, and other ocean animals. They also gathered berries, apples, and palm nuts to eat, and moss or plant fibers to make clothes.

Timucuans

The Timucuans moved into the central and northern regions and lived in villages led by powerful chiefs. Some experts believe that this group must have come from

ANCIENT LIVES

In 1984, archaeologists at the Windover Archaeological Dig in Titusville made some incredible finds. They excavated, or dug up, the oldest woven fabric found in North America, a bottle gourd, and other artifacts. Some of the skulls they found had fully intact brain tissue, and one woman's stomach contents were preserved. How is that possible? Oxygen helps living things decompose, or break down, after they die. Without oxygen, they can't break down. Peat bogs are places where the earth is so dense that no oxygen can get in. The area in Titusville had turned into a big peat bog over thousands of years. It is considered to be one of the most important archaeological digs in the world.

Want to know more? See www.nbbd.com/godo/history/windover/

Some Native Americans kept fruit and other food in large storage buildings.

Central or South America, because the group's language seems related to languages found that far south.

Apalachee

The Apalachee lived in the north and east areas of the Panhandle. The Appalachian Mountains, which run through this part of the continent, got their name from the Apalachee. The Apalachee grew corn, beans, pumpkins, and sunflowers. They hunted and fished and did a lot of trading. They also designed tools from stones, bones, and shells. They had a complex system of food storage. In fact, when European explorers came to the area, they found enough food to feed hundreds of people and horses for months.

Picture Yourself . . .

Looking in the Trash

Books are always telling you what archaeologists study and say, but did you ever wonder what an archaeologist actually does? Picture yourself digging through a pile of garbage. Why in the world would you want to do that? To find clues about the past. There aren't any ancient people around to tell you how they lived, so you need to figure it out. Discarded shell pieces can show you that the trash makers ate shellfish. Broken arrowheads give you hints about how ancient people hunted. Pottery shards can reveal what time they lived in, if you know how to date pottery. What will future archaeologists be able tell about you when they go through your garbage?

Tocobaga

Tampa Bay was home to the Tocobaga. Their homes were round and built with wooden poles. They piled mounds of shells and stones at their temple and their chief's home. Many scholars believe that the Tocobaga are responsible for developing a curved branch with a shell or stone on the end of it for digging, a tool called an *adze*.

Calusa

On the southwest coast were the Calusa. The men were especially tall and had long hair. Their homes were on stilts and had roofs but no walls. Unlike other groups, they did not farm, but instead relied on the ocean to provide food. They used the shells from their catches for making tools, jewelry, utensils, ornaments, and weapons, so they are sometimes called Shell Indians.

Until the early 1500s, these Native Americans had most of the peninsula to themselves. Their numbers had reached several hundred thousand. Communities were thriving with plenty of food, good weather, and a developing culture. This would all change with the arrival of the Europeans.

SEE IT HERE!

CRYSTAL RIVER ARCHAEOLOGICAL STATE PARK

On Florida's west coast, you'll find the Crystal River Archaeological State Park. This 61-acre (25-ha) Native American burial site has mounds, temples, and a plaza area. It was one of the longest continually inhabited places in the entire state. From about 200 BCE to 1400 CE, Crystal River was a very important place for Native Americans to hold ceremonies.

Archaeologists have found amazing clues to the past in more than 400 of these burial mounds. They have found many weapons and tools that were placed with the dead. Each one gives another glimpse into how these Native Americans once lived.

Knives made from animal bones.

WOW

The Calusa were great sailors. Their large canoes made of cypress logs were capable of reaching Cuba, and perhaps even Mexico.

READ ABOUT

When Ponce de León came to what is now Florida, he was searching for the fountain of youth.

1513
Juan Ponce de León lands on the shores of Florida

▲ 1539
Hernando de Soto comes to Florida with nine ships, 600 men, and 220 horses

1564
The Huguenots arrive from France and build a settlement

CHAPTER THREE

EXPLORATION AND SETTLEMENT

★

IN 1513, JUAN PONCE DE LEÓN LANDED ON THE SHORES OF FLORIDA, NORTH OF TODAY'S ST. AUGUSTINE. Earlier, this treasure seeker and explorer had lived on the Caribbean island of Hispaniola, which is today the countries of Haiti and the Dominican Republic, and had become the island's deputy governor. He came to Florida searching for gold, but he never found it.

1763 ►

The Treaty of Paris gives Florida to Britain in exchange for Cuba

1767

New Smyrna is founded by Greeks, Italians, and Minorcans

▲ **1783**

The American Revolution ends

TRYING TO CLAIM FLORIDA

Ponce de León instead saw beautiful land and countless islands. Eventually, he ran into the Calusa people, who chased him and his men back to their ships. He spent the next few years exploring other areas and temporarily settled in Puerto Rico. Finally, in 1521, determined to claim Florida for Spain, he returned, ready to **colonize** it. He brought supplies, weapons, missionaries, and settlers with him—everything he needed to ensure victory. The Calusa defended themselves, fearing Ponce de León and his men would take their land and supplies. They shot Ponce de León with a poisoned arrow. He fled with his men and later died from his wound in Cuba at the age of 61.

For the next 40 years, others followed Ponce de León's example. They came to Florida to create a colony and were defeated one by one—by Native Americans, stormy weather, unexpected illness, the harsh wilderness, or a combination of these factors. In 1528, Pánfilo

WORD TO KNOW

colonize *to establish a colony, which is a new settlement with ties to another governing state*

FLORIDA PLACE NAMES

Imagine if you were in a place that nobody had ever made a map of before. You would need to come up with names for all the different features of the landscape, so you and your friends could find each other in it. Ponce de León is responsible for several of the place names still used in Florida today. Cape Canaveral, which means "cape of currents," was named for the rough waters he encountered when he sailed through this area. He named one island Dry Tortugas because there was no freshwater there, but there were plenty of turtles—or *tortugas*. He called the Keys Los Martires, which means "martyred men."

Want to know more? See www.floridahistory.org/floridians/conquis.htm

Hernando de Soto and his expedition landing in Florida in 1539.

de Narváez landed at Tampa Bay with 400 men. They were looking for gold in the Panhandle region, but between disease and raids by the Calusa, few of them survived long enough to leave Florida's shores.

In 1539, explorer Hernando de Soto arrived in Florida with 10 ships and more than 600 soldiers, 24 priests, and fellow explorers. He also brought pigs, dogs, and 220 horses. They managed to stay for four years, searching for that ever-elusive gold and coming into contact with many Native Americans. Few Europeans survived, and de Soto himself died of fever, in what is now Arkansas, in 1542.

Two decades after de Soto, Tristán de Luna y Arellano sailed into Pensacola Bay with 1,500 soldiers, priests, and craftspeople determined to set up a Spanish settlement. They ran out of food, battled the local tribes, and after a hurricane hit in 1561, they left.

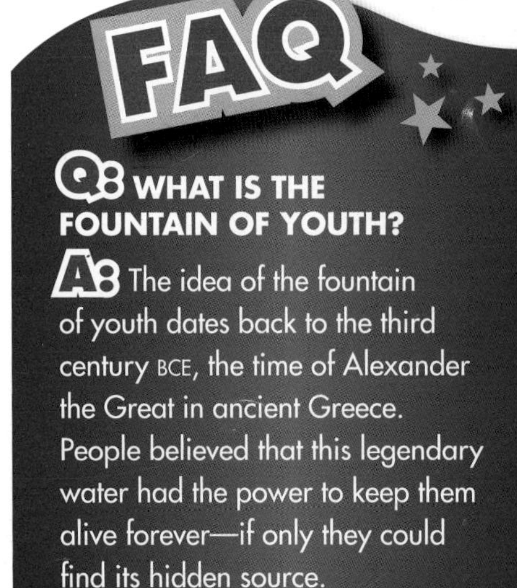

FAQ
Q: WHAT IS THE FOUNTAIN OF YOUTH?
A: The idea of the fountain of youth dates back to the third century BCE, the time of Alexander the Great in ancient Greece. People believed that this legendary water had the power to keep them alive forever—if only they could find its hidden source.

European Exploration of Florida

The colored arrows on this map show the routes taken by explorers between 1513 and 1543.

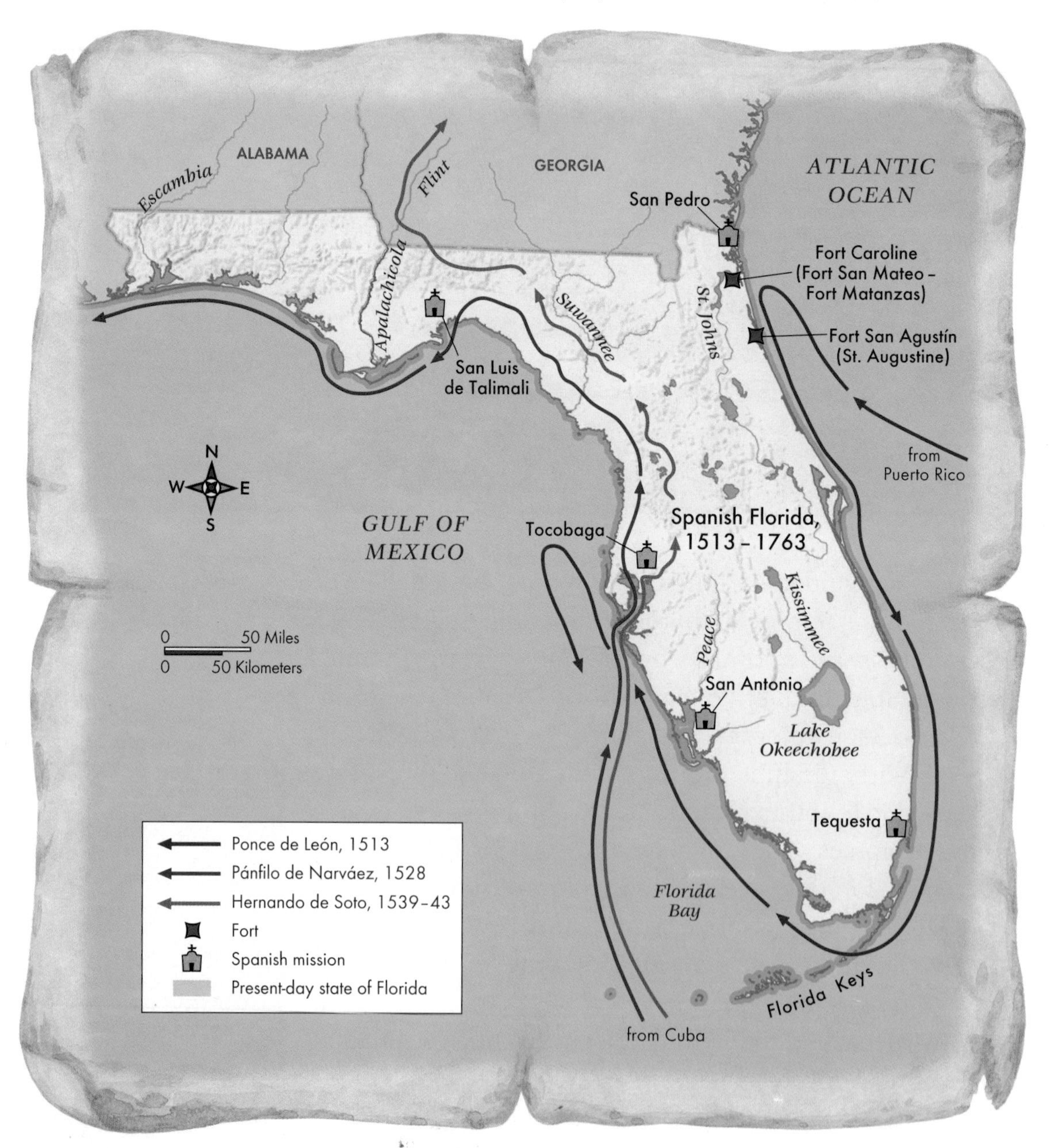

THE HUGUENOTS

In 1564, a new obstacle stood in the way of Spain's controlling the land. A French group called Huguenots had left their home country in search of religious freedom and arrived in Florida. Finding the land to be rich, they built a settlement called Fort Caroline near today's Jacksonville.

In order to sustain their existence, they devised a plan. They would lie in wait for Spanish ships to go by and attack them for the cargo they carried. Often the Spanish ships were full of gold, silver, copper, and precious stones. The French pirates would attack and then quickly retreat into the thick mangrove swamps or to one of the many little islands in the Keys.

Needless to say, Spain was annoyed. The Huguenots were disrupting trade. And they were getting in the way of Spain's mission to spread the Catholic religion around the world.

In 1565, King Philip II sent Captain Pedro Menéndez de Avilés to Florida to drive out the Huguenots. He succeeded, but not for long. Over the next two centuries, many Europeans arrived in colonial Florida—including Catholic and Protestant Irish, Italians, Jews, Scots, English, and more French Huguenots and Spaniards. Loosely governed by Spain, the peninsula became a home to all kinds of people seeking refuge.

Spanish gold coins

Picture Yourself . . .

On a Pirate Ship

Life on a pirate ship may sound like it was fun, but it was usually a lot of hard work. And frequently, your life was at risk from either the battles on the ships you were raiding or just the dangers of the unpredictable sea itself. There were many different jobs onboard these ships. Keeping watch, making repairs, cooking food, cleaning the decks, washing dishes, stowing provisions, shifting cargo, and handing out punishment were all common chores. The youngest and newest sailors were called apprentice seamen, and they usually got the chores no one else wanted.

MINI-BIO

FRANCISCO MENENDEZ: FORT DEFENDER

In 1728 Florida officials asked African Francisco Menendez (dates unknown), an escaped slave, to command a fort designed to protect St. Augustine. Captain Menendez brought dozens of fellow Africans to the fort, where they planted crops, attended church, and promised to defend Spain. As news of the fort spread, more runaways fled their chains, and the settlement grew. Known as Fort Mose, it was the first free black settlement in America.

Menendez and his people were a vital part of Spanish Florida's history and defense.

ARRIVAL OF AFRICAN LABORERS

From the early 1700s, Spain imported Africans to perform their colony's hard work. African labor built St. Augustine, first as a garrison and then as a town. African families attended and were married in its churches, and the men served in Florida's militia. Many Africans, slave and free, brought special skills. Some quickly learned European and Indian languages, and they were hired to serve as interpreters, negotiators, and diplomats. Northwestern Africans were rice-planting experts.

An intense military rivalry arose between Catholic Spain and Protestant England, which helped some enslaved Africans to obtain freedom. Spanish governors offered liberty to slaves who escaped from the southern British colonies. They recruited Africans to attack British plantations and settlements in the Carolinas. These Africans often returned with people they had freed, sometimes their own relatives. When the British demanded their return, Spanish officials not only refused, but they hired the men and women as workers and converted them to Catholicism. Eventually the Spanish Crown offered freedom to all runaways from the British who accepted Catholicism as the "true faith."

Increasingly, slaves fled the British colonies to accept Spanish hospitality and liberty. By 1746 people

This is a view of St. Augustine in 1763. In the years to come, the town was home to a growing population of Africans, Indians, and Spaniards.

of African descent, many mixed with Indians and Spaniards, were one-fourth of St. Augustine's 1,500 residents. Many joined the Catholic Church, which welcomed them with open arms. By 1763 the peninsula's black population rose to 3,000, and one in four was free.

STRUGGLE FOR CONTROL

In 1763, the tug of war between Spain and Britain for control of Florida came to an end, when Spain gave Florida to England (without permission from its original inhabitants). Africans fled to Cuba rather than face retaliation or enslavement.

SLAVERY IN FLORIDA

Most slaves toiled long hours as field workers, while some were cooks and servants in their owners' mansions. Still others performed skilled crafts, and some held positions of trust and management. There were good masters and bad, and not all slaves were beaten. But enslaved family members could be and were sold separately. Planters in Florida and other slave states said the enslaved were "the happiest and best provided for workers in the world." Squires Jackson, a freed Florida slave, disagreed: "Even the best masters in slavery couldn't be as good as the worst person in Freedom. Oh, God, it's good to be free."

The British divided Florida into east and west to make governing it more manageable. The capital city in the east was St. Augustine and in the west was Pensacola. The British brought African slaves on ships to work their orchards and fields of figs, cotton, indigo, sugarcane, and rice.

Many Europeans and Africans were killed in the battles for control of Florida, but the largest group of victims in these ongoing battles was the Native Americans. Each time the British came ashore to fight, they left with hundreds of Native Americans to sell as slaves in the British colonies. European diseases such as measles and smallpox were devastating to Native Americans, who could no longer fend off the Europeans as the Calusa once had.

In 1742, British troops led a surprise attack against Spanish forces.

Under the leadership of Bernardo de Gálvez, Spanish troops captured Pensacola from the British in 1781.

Many new arrivals in British-ruled Florida were not English. In 1767, a group of 200 Greeks, 110 Italians, and more than 1,000 Minorcans (from Spain) founded New Smyrna. Under harsh conditions, these settlers worked hard, building homes and producing food, particularly olives.

With the American Revolution (1775–1783), control of Florida changed hands again. Florida did its best to stay out of the fight, but it still depended on Britain for money. Since many of Florida's soldiers were fighting elsewhere, Spain decided it would be a good time to sneak in. In 1781, they landed in West Florida at Pensacola and captured it without much resistance. Soon after the war ended, Spain took control of East Florida as well.

The Seminole of the Everglades lived in homes made of thatch.

THE SEMINOLE TAKE SHAPE

Around the time of the American Revolution, the Seminole (whose name means "runaway") fled their homes in Georgia and Alabama. They were trying to escape unfair treatment by the Creek. In Florida they were welcomed by the colonies of African slave runaways living there. The Africans then taught the newcomers methods of rice cultivation they had brought from their homelands of Senegambia and Sierra Leone.

Some Africans and Seminole married, but other Africans lived in separate villages. The Seminole were determined to use force against anyone who tried to take their land or seize their people as slaves. Africans, beginning as Seminole interpreters and diplomats, soon rose to leadership in the new Seminole Nation. They had more to lose by an invasion: not just their land, but their freedom as well.

Florida's Seminole Nation shone as a beacon of liberty to enslaved people. But slaveholders, especially in Georgia, Alabama, and the Carolinas, saw the Seminole as a dangerous threat. It wasn't long before the U.S. government would get involved—and war would break out.

SEE IT HERE!

THE AH-TAH-THI-KI MUSEUM

There is so much to learn about the Seminole. So plan a visit to the Ah-Tah-Thi-Ki Museum, which is located on the Seminole's Big Cypress Reservation in the Florida Everglades. It features the nation's largest display of the life and culture of the Florida Seminole through exhibits, rare artifacts, and cultural displays. Learn about canoes made of cypress trees and see how the Seminole survived by farming and hunting. You can also experience an authentic Native American village with Seminole members preparing traditional arts and crafts. And get a glimpse into the annual Green Corn Dance, a sacred religious ceremony.

Want to know more? See www.seminoletribe.com/museum/

Among their many rituals, the Seminole participated in the Green Corn Dance.

READ ABOUT

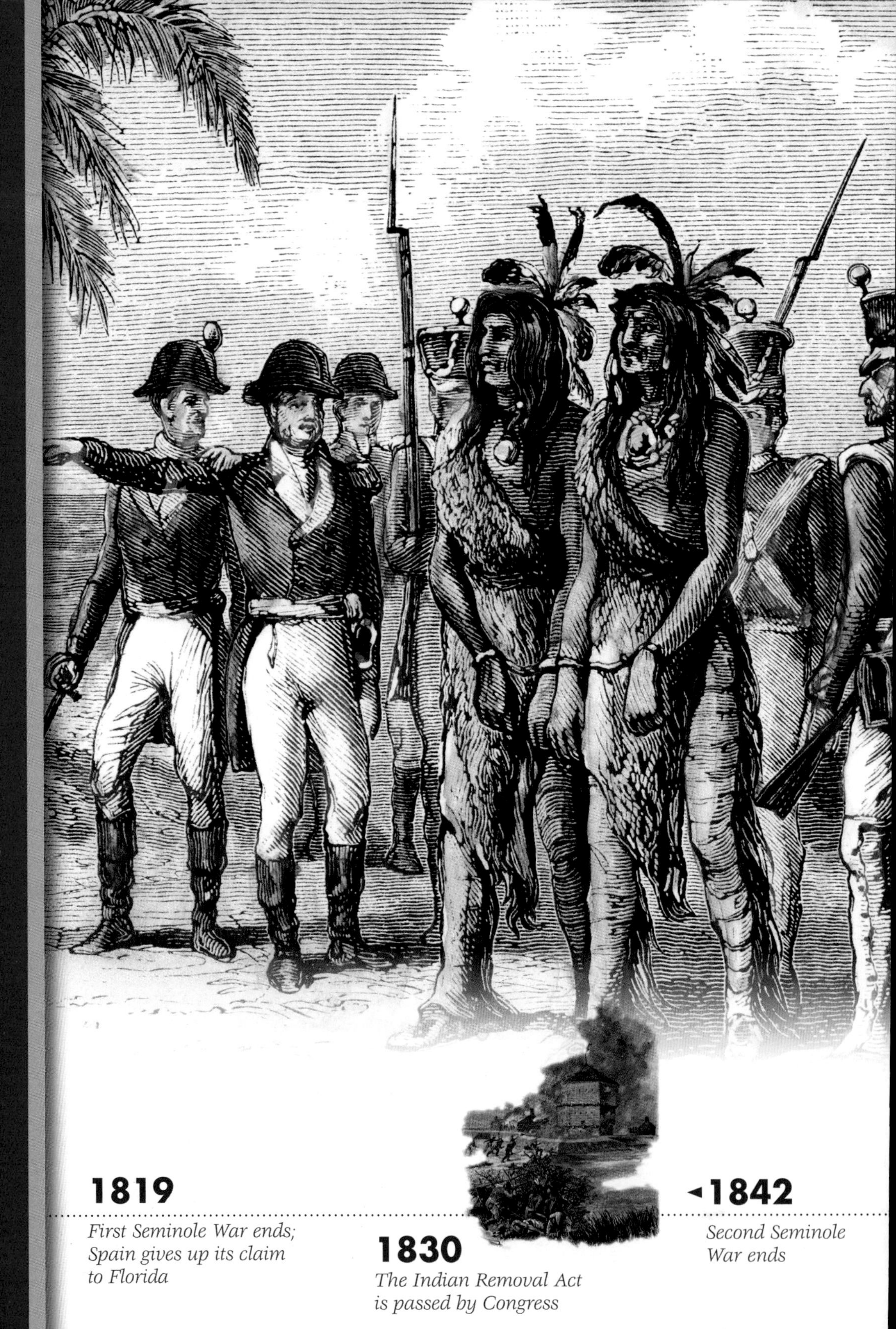

The capture of Seminole chiefs during the First Seminole War

1819
First Seminole War ends; Spain gives up its claim to Florida

1830
The Indian Removal Act is passed by Congress

1842
Second Seminole War ends

CHAPTER FOUR

GROWTH AND CHANGE

THE SEMINOLE NATION PROVIDED REFUGE TO RUNAWAY SLAVES FROM SOUTHERN STATES. So slave catchers began crossing into Florida from Georgia. Then U.S. authorities began forcing their way into Seminole villages in search of slaves, as well. The U.S. battle to control the Seminole heated up, and both sides stood firm.

1845
Florida becomes a state

1858
Third Seminole War ends

1868
Florida holds a constitutional convention

A group of Seminole preparing to ambush U.S. troops near Fort Scott in 1817.

THE FIRST SEMINOLE WAR

In 1817, the First Seminole War began. Months later, General Andrew Jackson and more than 3,000 soldiers thundered into Florida and attacked the Seminole.

Two years later, Spain finally gave up its claim to Florida. In turn, the United States canceled the $5 million debt that the Spanish had owed them.

In 1823, driven by an endless desire for more land and a generally **bigoted** attitude about Indians, American soldiers and settlers tried and failed to force the Seminole to move to a reservation in central Florida. Seven years later, in 1830, Congress passed the Indian Removal Act, which President Andrew Jackson signed into law. The U.S. government forcibly moved thousands of eastern Indians from their native lands to areas in the West. Their long and difficult march is called the Trail of Tears.

WORD TO KNOW

bigoted *having unfair opinions of a group, based on that group's religion, race, or other factors*

THE SECOND SEMINOLE WAR

The Second Seminole War began in 1835 when a Seminole named Osceola killed an American official, and Seminole warriors ambushed American troops near Ocala. Around this time, two young Seminole men became friends when they united to fight the United States. Wild Cat, or Coacoochee, was a good negotiator. John Horse, or John Cohia, was of African descent, and a masterful diplomat. Together they led **guerrilla** armies, moving Seminole families out of harm's way as they did, and negotiating peace terms with their foes.

In 1837, American soldiers captured the friends along with ten other Seminole. The group of 12 men and women made a spectacular escape from Fort Marion and fled southward and rallied their fighting forces. Pursued by Colonel Zachary Scott Taylor and more than 1,000 troops, the Seminole fled to Lake Okeechobee, where

WORD TO KNOW

guerrilla *describing soldiers who don't belong to regular armies; they often use surprise attacks and other uncommon battle tactics*

Seminole Indians, led by Osceola, attacking Fort King in 1837

THE SEMINOLE IN MEXICO

In 1849, Seminole leaders Wild Cat and John Horse, fearful of slave catchers capturing their people, led a massive exodus from Indian Territory (present-day Oklahoma) to Texas. As posses opened fire, the Seminole men managed to ferry their women and children safely across the Rio Grande. The Seminole Nation settled in Mexico. In return for land and wages, young Seminole men served the Mexican government as border guards. In 20 years at the border, the Seminole fought many battles, but never lost a person or had one seriously wounded.

MINI-BIO

OSCEOLA: SEMINOLE LEADER

Born just after the turn of the 19th century, Osceola (1804–1838) was first known as Little Owl. He moved with his family to northern Florida as a child and joined the Seminole tribe there. He tried to prevent the Native Americans from losing their land to the white settlers.

In 1837, during the Second Seminole War, Osceola went to General Thomas Jesup's fort and approached holding a white flag of surrender. He and his people were tired of fighting. The general's men surrounded him, threw his flag on the ground, bound him in chains, and put him in prison. While there, the famous painter George Catlin came to visit him. Catlin later wrote, "This gallant fellow is grieving with a broken spirit, and ready to die, cursing the white man, no doubt to the end of his breath." The two became friends, and Catlin painted Osceola's portrait (shown above). Days after it was finished, Osceola died of malaria at age 34.

Want to know more? See www.seminoletribe.com/history/osceola-abiaka.shtml

their sharpshooters waited in trees and in the tall grass. As Taylor's forces approached, pinpoint Seminole gunfire brought down nearly all the troops. As night fell, Wild Cat, John Horse, and their soldiers escaped across the lake. Taylor claimed victory, but the United States had suffered its worst Indian defeat.

THE THIRD SEMINOLE WAR

The third war between the U.S. government and the Seminole began in 1855 and was known as the Billy Bowlegs War. Billy was actually Olactomico, a Seminole chief and one of the only remaining leaders. After being attacked repeatedly and hunted down with bloodhounds, Billy surrendered in May 1858.

The three Seminole wars at times tied up half of the U.S. Army, led to 1,500 U.S. combat deaths, and caused Congress to spend more than $30 million. Finally, most Seminole agreed to move to Indian Territory. But some stayed in Florida, never gave up their land, and never surrendered. Today, more than 2,000 Seminole live on reservations in Hollywood, Big Cypress, Brighton, Immokalee, Fort Pierce, and Tampa.

Florida: From Territory to Statehood

(1822–1845)

This map shows the original Florida territory (outlined in red and green) and the area (in yellow) that became the state of Florida in 1845.

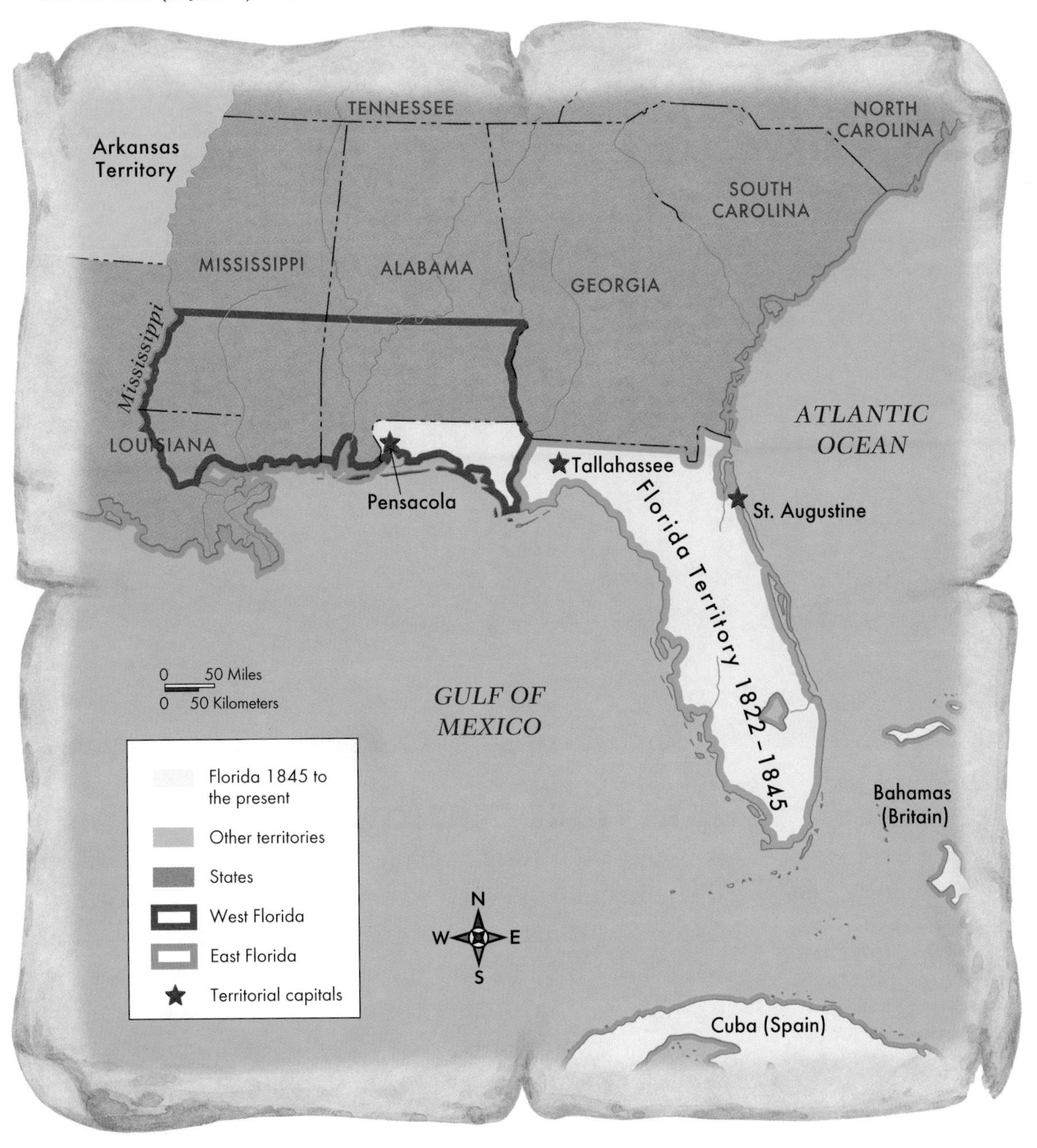

Confederate soldiers at Fort McRee. These troops trained in Florida and fought during the Civil War.

Not everyone in the South was a Confederate during the Civil War. Key West remained loyal to the North and became an active post for Union soldiers.

A DIVIDED NATION

Not long after the Seminole Wars ended, another conflict emerged: the Civil War. In March 1845, Florida had become the nation's 27th state. As a Southern state, with more than 63,000 slaves, it was a member of the Confederacy. Although few actual battles were fought in Florida, the state's main job was supplying meat, salt, and sugar to the Confederate troops.

RECONSTRUCTION

When the war ended and the Confederacy was defeated in 1865, more than 40,000 enslaved people in the state were freed. Florida's planters resented losing their free labor supply, and many hoped to restore slavery. African Americans were thankful they could now work for themselves and their families. Former slaves, looking forward to using their new rights after the Civil War, were on a collision course with their former masters, many of whom would make it difficult for blacks to actually enjoy those rights.

In 1868, Florida drafted a new state constitution. Some 59 percent of voters were African American men. And of the 46 delegates who would write the new constitution, 18 were African Americans, including former slaves. Some poor whites sided with black delegates who favored equal rights and public schools. A long struggle to choose the path Floridians would take toward a fair government began.

MINI-BIO

JAMES WELDON JOHNSON: POET AND CIVIL RIGHTS ACTIVIST

James Weldon Johnson (1871–1938) was born in Jacksonville, Florida, and educated by his mother and the **segregated** public schools. He graduated college and founded a newspaper that attacked racial prejudice.

In celebration of Lincoln's birthday in 1900, James and his brother, Rosamond, wrote "Lift Every Voice and Sing," and black children in Jacksonville sang it at their school assembly. The song became famous as the Negro National Anthem, sung wherever African Americans gathered. Johnson became a noted attorney, author, poet, novelist, diplomat, songwriter, civil rights activist, and leader of the National Association for the Advancement of Colored People (NAACP).

Want to know more? See *Words of Promise: A Story About James Weldon Johnson* by Jodie A. Shull (Minneapolis: Millbrook Press, 2005)

WORD TO KNOW

segregated *separated from others, based on race, class, ethnic group, or other factors*

A NEW CENTURY DAWNS

By the turn of the 20th century, much of Florida was still wetlands. People could neither build nor plant on it, so the land was sold very cheaply—sometimes even given away—to those who had the funds to drain it and start construction. A great deal of this land went to railroad companies. These companies were eager to set up a transportation system that would ship growing amounts of produce to states in the North.

One businessman who helped Florida grow was Vicente Ybor. He moved to Key West from Cuba and established a cigar-making company. He later moved to Tampa and built a factory called Ybor City. Ybor hired thousands of workers and forged friendships throughout the community. In 1896, Ybor died, but his business continued. And by 1900, Ybor City was called the Cigar Capital of the World.

Florida began to change dramatically. People all over the country were becoming aware of the state's sunny weather, resources, and potential for tourism. It wasn't long before businesspeople with deep pockets and grand notions began flooding the area. They were ready to take advantage of the lack of development by providing their own—and making millions in the process.

The arrival of the Orange Blossom Special in Ft. Lauderdale, in about 1921.

MINI-BIO

HENRY FLAGLER: FLORIDA MILLIONAIRE

On honeymoon with his second wife in St. Augustine, Henry Flagler (1830–1913) saw the need for better facilities for Florida's visitors. He and John D. Rockefeller had become millionaires with their founding of the Standard Oil Company. Flagler decided to focus his time and money on developing hotels, as well as purchasing railroads, so that tourists could get to Florida faster and easier.

He began building a railroad that would give people access to the southern half of Florida. His projects kept getting bigger and more impressive. He built numerous hotels and expanded his railways in all directions. He even extended a railway across the water, all the way to Key West.

Want to know more? See flaglermuseum.us/html/flagler_biography.html

READ ABOUT

Visitors to the Roney Plaza Hotel in Miami Beach during the 1950s. Many hotels were built during this time to accommodate the growing number of tourists to the area.

1929
The Great Depression begins

▲ 1960s
Waves of Cuban immigrants begin coming to Florida

1964
Martin Luther King Jr. visits Florida

MORE MODERN TIMES

★

FOR DECADES, NOT MANY PEOPLE LIVED IN FLORIDA COMPARED TO OTHER STATES. Then air-conditioning came along. Suddenly, people could get relief from the heat in the summer months. As the 20th century began, Florida got busy. Ambitious businesspeople built hotels and railroads, farmers planted oranges, and tourists headed south to enjoy the warm weather in the winter months. Florida was thriving.

1969
Launched from the Kennedy Space Center, Apollo 11 *lands on the moon*

1987 ►
Bob Martinez becomes the first Latino governor of the state

2004
Four hurricanes hit Florida

SEE IT HERE!

CORAL CASTLE

Ed Leedskalnin stood only 5 feet tall (1.5 m) and weighed a mere 100 pounds (45 kg). But he somehow built a castle out of 2.2 million pounds (998,000 kg) of coral rock all by himself. Leedskalnin built this huge place to impress the 16-year-old bride who had left him at the altar. It is located in Homestead and is known as the Coral Castle.

Leedskalnin took 20 years to complete the castle (1920–1940). In 1953, two years after he died, the place opened as a tourist attraction. Guests are amazed by the front gate, which weighs 9 tons and yet can be opened by the slight push of one finger. Inside, they marvel at the stone telescope that is permanently pointed toward the North Star.

FACING DISASTER

Just as Florida was enjoying its growth, everything changed. In 1926, a powerful hurricane whipped through the state, catching Floridians off guard. A second major hurricane hit in 1928. Within two years, these storms killed more than 2,000 people. Floridians were beginning to recover when another disaster struck. The stock market crashed in October 1929, and the nation plunged deeper into the Great Depression. Banks closed, and people lost their jobs and life savings. In Florida, the money for hotels and railroad tracks disappeared. Those people who previously had money to take vacations now spent it just to put food on the table.

The Miami coastline was hit hard by a hurricane on October 21, 1926.

These crewmen are securing an airship at Banana River Naval Air Station, 1943. Florida was a major center for training troops during World War II.

MAKING A COMEBACK

World War II (1939–1945) was the most widespread and destructive war in history. Ironically, this terrible event also helped pull the nation out of the Great Depression. In Florida, shipyards put people to work building more than 100 Liberty warships. Florida became home to a number of U.S. military bases. The government built hotels to house soldiers and used them as training camps and hospitals, too. Air force pilots practiced takeoffs and landings on Florida's open land. The government sped up construction of highways and airports to handle the military's comings and goings.

Between 1945 and 1954, there were more hotel rooms built in Miami than in the rest of the United States put together.

THE CIVIL RIGHTS MOVEMENT

After World War II, Florida lawmakers turned their attention from military to educational matters. They needed to strengthen the state's education system for a couple of reasons. One was to make Florida more attractive to new businesses. More important, they needed to improve black schools to meet the federal court's

In 1956, the people of Tallahassee boycotted the city bus system for its unfair treatment of African American riders. Brodus Hartley (right) led students at Florida A & M University in the protest.

recent demands for fair and equal public education. So the legislature created the Minimum Foundations Program for public schools.

Some white groups resisted this program, not wanting African Americans to have equal rights. The Ku Klux Klan was the most prominent group, and many of its members committed violent crimes against blacks. Sometimes African Americans who complained or spoke out about unfair wages or work conditions were put in jail.

Harry T. Moore, along with his wife, Harriette, was one of the United States' most recognized and dedicated civil rights workers. Born in Houston, Florida, Moore helped to organize the first Brevard County, Florida, branch of the National Association for the Advancement of Colored People (NAACP), in 1934. As the executive secretary of the Progressive Voters League, he helped to register tens of thousands of black Americans in Florida. He also helped the county appoint its first black deputy sheriff, in 1950. The Ku Klux Klan murdered Moore and his wife in 1951.

But the Moores did not die in vain. In 1954, the Supreme Court ruled in *Brown v. the Board of Education* that segregation in U.S. public schools was illegal. For years, there had been separate water fountains, bathrooms, restaurant seating, and hotel rooms for whites and blacks. But those restrictions began to disappear with the Supreme Court's historic ruling. In May 1956, two black women sat in the front seats of a Tallahassee bus even though the law stated that they should sit in the back. When white authorities arrested them, the entire African American community began a **boycott** of the bus system. This protest led the legislature to revise many racist laws and policies.

In 1964, Dr. Martin Luther King Jr. visited Florida. He promoted peaceful protests and organized groups to march for civil rights. One of these marches took place in St. Augustine in June of that year. There were many violent outbursts and fights between the marchers and bystanders who were against **integration**. But this event led the way for more marches. Eventually, the Civil Rights Act of 1964 outlawed segregation.

The civil rights movement influenced other groups, as well. The Seminole Indians created a constitution in 1957 that was designed to protect their civil rights and land ownership in Florida. This action helped make Floridians aware of the history of the Seminole and their contributions to Florida.

WORDS TO KNOW

boycott *the organized refusal to use a service or buy a product, as a form of protest*

integration *the incorporation of all races and groups into society; the opposite of segregation*

MINI-BIO

BETTY MAE TIGER JUMPER: THE FIRST FLORIDA SEMINOLE GRADUATE

She was determined to graduate from high school. But as the daughter of a full-blooded Seminole mother and a white father, Betty Mae Tiger Jumper (1922–) knew that her choices in the Everglades were limited. At that time, Native American children could not go to Florida schools. Instead, Betty Mae, her brother, and a cousin traveled more than 1,000 miles (1,600 km) to an Indian reservation in North Carolina. There they went to school and became the first Florida Seminoles to receive high school diplomas. Later, Betty Mae came back to Florida and established a tribal newsletter. In 1967, she was elected head of the Seminole Tribal Council, the first woman to hold this position.

Want to know more? See www.upf.com/fall2001/jumper.html

In the 1960s, Florida's large Hispanic community worked for equal rights, as well. Hispanics pushed for opportunities in higher education and greater involvement in politics and government. In 1979, Robert "Bob" Martinez became mayor of Tampa. In 1987, he became Florida's first Latino governor.

FLORIDA'S SPACE PROGRAM

In 1949, the U.S. government was testing missiles at Cape Canaveral Air Force Station. In 1958, Congress created the National Aeronautics and Space Administration (NASA), and U.S. Air Force crews launched missiles for NASA from Cape Canaveral. As the years passed, missile testing at the station ended and it became the nation's center for launching rockets and shuttles into space.

In 1962, President John F. Kennedy gave a speech vowing that Americans would walk on the moon by the end of the decade. "We choose to go to the moon," he declared, ". . . not because [it is] easy, but because [it is] hard . . ." In 1962, the Launch Operations Center was opened at Cape Canaveral. After President Kennedy's death in 1963, this facility was renamed the John F. Kennedy Space Center.

The space shuttle *Discovery* at liftoff in 1988. It launched the Hubble Space Telescope two years later.

In 1969, millions of Americans sat riveted to their televisions as *Apollo 11* lifted off from Florida and landed on the moon. Just three years later, President Richard Nixon announced the country's intention to develop a space shuttle program for traveling into space. The first shuttle was tested successfully in 1981. The following year, a shuttle with a four-astronaut crew took off. Shuttle missions continued until 1986, when the *Challenger* exploded 73 seconds after liftoff, killing all seven crew members. *Discovery* marked the return to space in 1988, and it docked with *Mir*, the Russian space station, in 1995. Other space shuttles include *Endeavour*, which serviced the Hubble Space Telescope in 1993. Today, shuttles continue to explore space.

Between 1950 and 1999, more than 3,000 missiles, rockets, and crewed space vehicles made launches from the Kennedy Space Center.

A street mural in Miami's Little Havana neighborhood. Written on it are the words *Viva nuestra raza!*, which mean "Our race lives!" in Spanish.

A CHANGING POPULATION

Warm weather, good job growth, and a fairly low cost of living lured new residents to Florida in the early 1960s. The state's population climbed quickly. Between 1950 and 1960, the space program caused the population of Brevard County to explode more than 370 percent. Winter tourists were also coming in growing numbers.

In addition, a revolution in Cuba in 1959 led thousands of its residents to move to nearby Florida. When Fidel Castro, the new Cuban leader, began taking away their freedom, many Cuban citizens decided to start a new life in Miami and other Florida cities. In 1965 alone, 100,000 Cubans packed into the twice-daily "freedom flights" between Havana and Miami. Many of these people settled in the Riverside section of Miami, and that area was soon called Little Havana (after the capital of Cuba).

In the years to come, Cuban immigrants arrived in Florida in waves. In 1980, the Mariel Boatlift—a mass exodus of Cubans from Mariel Harbor, Cuba—brought 150,000 Cubans to Miami. Also in the 1980s, thousands of people from impoverished Haiti came to Florida by boat. Some traveled in makeshift boats. Many others, aboard vessels that were little more than flimsy rafts, lost their lives at sea. Nevertheless, others followed, believing a new life in America was worth the risk. Before long, the U.S. government started placing restrictions on the number of Haitians and Cubans who could come to the United States.

In the 21st century, Miami has become a popular destination for immigrants and tourists alike. The city's rich cultural mosaic is appealing to people from all over the world.

WHAT THE FUTURE HOLDS

In 1992, the second-most destructive hurricane in U.S. history struck the shores of south Florida. Floridians who were hit by Hurricane Andrew had to pick up the pieces and rebuild. Twelve years later, in 2004, four hurricanes—Charley, Frances, Ivan, and Jeanne—made landfall in the Sunshine State. It was a harrowing few months for Florida residents as they tried to recover between storms. But these disasters have not discouraged them.

As the population grows, the state faces a number of challenges. It needs to build more schools to accommodate all its new residents. It needs to build bigger and better roads to handle all the new traffic. And it needs to create well-planned communities as more and more houses are built. The state has to continue to educate its residents about hurricanes and how to be protected during severe storms. The people of Florida have weathered enormous changes. And they are ready for whatever lies ahead.

READ ABOUT

Sponge cutter George Billiris at work in his factory in Tarpon Springs

CHAPTER SIX

PEOPLE

★

WALKING THROUGH THE STREETS OF TARPON SPRINGS, YOU MAY NOTICE THE SWEET AROMA OF GREEK PASTRIES AND THE SALTY SCENT OF SEA SPONGES DRYING IN THE SUNSHINE. You would think you were in Greece, along the Aegean coast. Actually, you are in central Florida, where Greek divers came a century ago to harvest sponges from the ocean and build a community. Tarpon Springs is just one example of a Florida town with a distinct ethnic flavor.

A big crowd enjoying the Fourth of July festivities in Miami

People QuickFacts

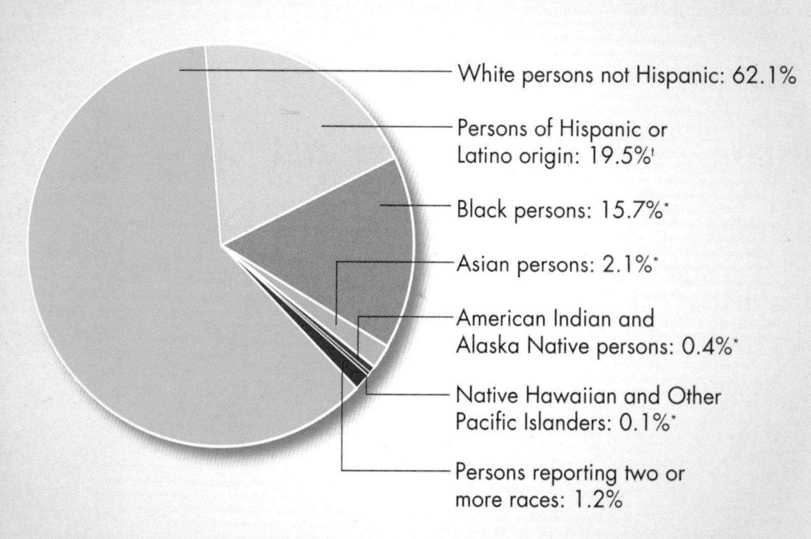

*Includes persons reporting only one race
†Hispanics may be of any race, so they are also included in applicable race categories.
Source: U.S. Census Bureau, 2005 estimate

PEOPLE FROM ALL OVER

Floridians come from all over the place, especially from Haiti, Cuba, Puerto Rico, Mexico, and many U.S. states. In fact, one in 10 Floridians comes from another state. Some are people who visited and decided to relocate. Some are retirees who want to live in a warm, sunny place.

No single ethnic group dominates Florida's population. Miami-Dade is the only county in the entire country

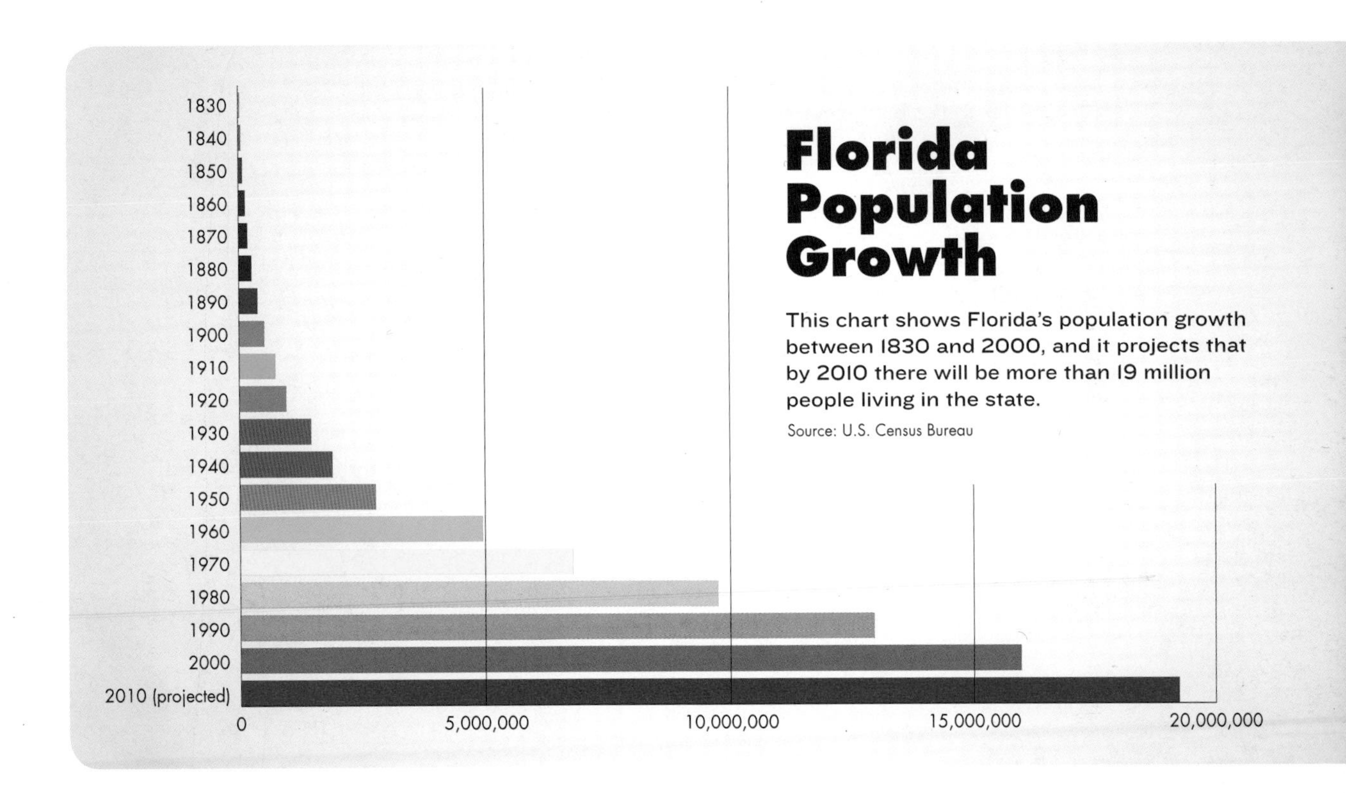

Florida Population Growth

This chart shows Florida's population growth between 1830 and 2000, and it projects that by 2010 there will be more than 19 million people living in the state.

Source: U.S. Census Bureau

where more than half the people were not born in the United States. Most are from Cuba, Colombia, Haiti, Nicaragua, Jamaica, and Mexico. Although Florida's African American population has been declining in recent years, many African American communities still thrive in north central Florida and in the Everglades region.

Miami's Little Havana neighborhood is home to a bustling Cuban community. Latin music drifts out of storefronts, and the smell of strong coffee and spicy foods wafts along the streets and sidewalks. Vendors offer tastes of *chicharones,* or fried pork morsels, and drinks of *guarapo,* or sweet sugarcane juice, to wash them down.

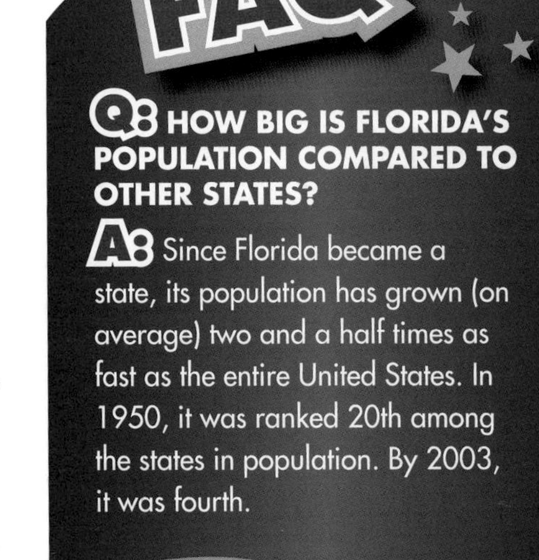

Q HOW BIG IS FLORIDA'S POPULATION COMPARED TO OTHER STATES?

A Since Florida became a state, its population has grown (on average) two and a half times as fast as the entire United States. In 1950, it was ranked 20th among the states in population. By 2003, it was fourth.

Where Floridians Live

The colors on this map indicate population density throughout the state. The darker the color, the more people live there.

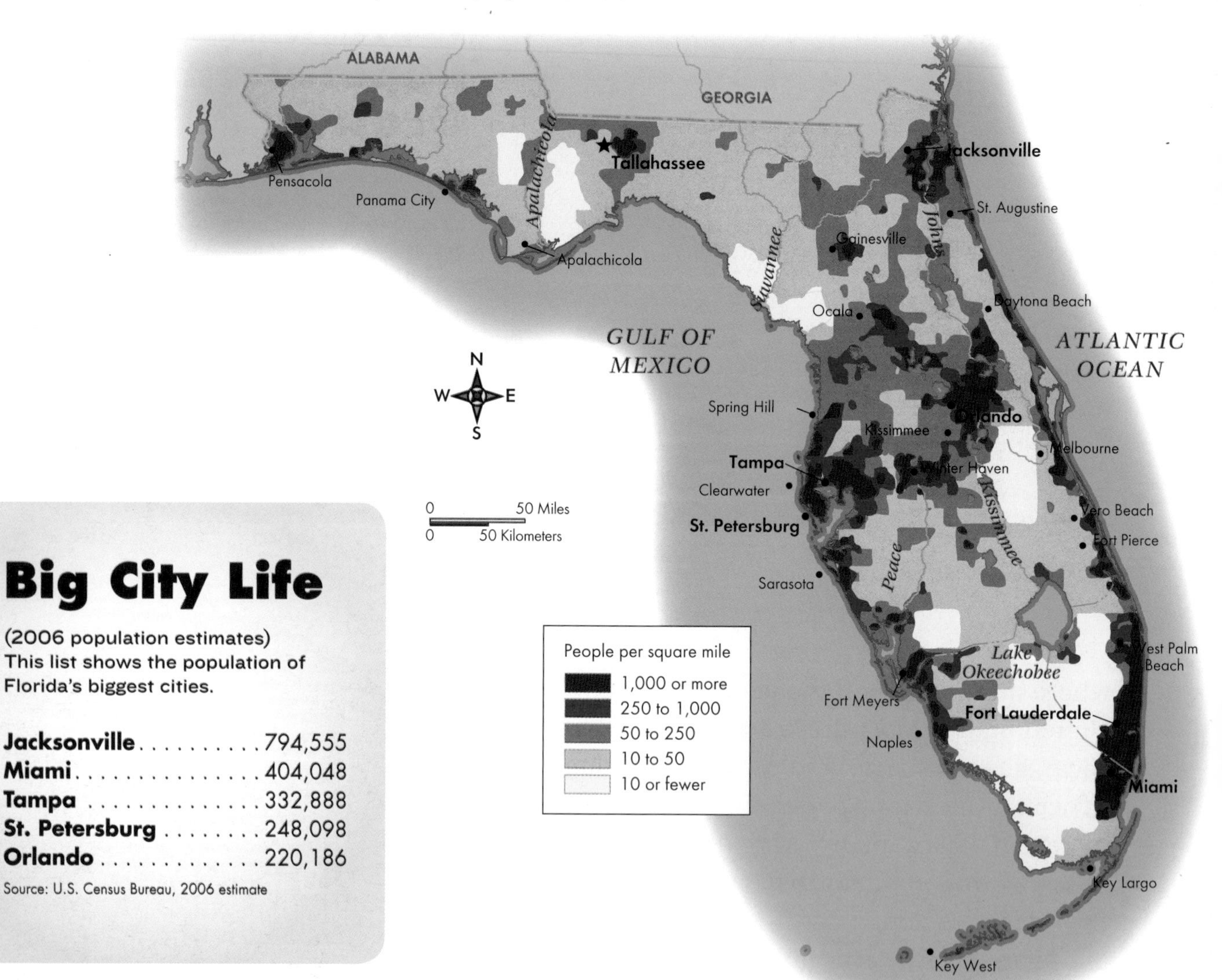

Big City Life

(2006 population estimates)
This list shows the population of Florida's biggest cities.

Jacksonville	794,555
Miami	404,048
Tampa	332,888
St. Petersburg	248,098
Orlando	220,186

Source: U.S. Census Bureau, 2006 estimate

The population of Florida's Flagler County grew from 49,832 in 2000 to 76,410 in 2005. That's 53 percent in just five years, making it the fastest growing county in the country.

The skyline of Jacksonville, Florida's most-populated city

TOWN AND COUNTRY

About 90 percent of Floridians live in the state's biggest cities, which are mainly found on the coasts. Jacksonville is the biggest one of all. A lot of little neighborhoods, each one with its own style, make up the huge city of Miami. A blend of distinct ethnic neighborhoods and communities make Miami unlike any other city in the world.

But Florida is not just about cities. Small towns include fishing villages such as Sebastian and Boca Grande. And orange groves can be seen for miles throughout the state. Ocala is horse country. It boasts more than 400 horse farms.

People from all over the world come to Florida to enjoy the sun and surf, as well as to relax or retire. They, however, make up only a small portion of the population. Most of the people in the state get up and go to work like everyone else in the nation. Almost three-quarters of them are on the service end of the vacation scene. They are the ones serving the food, taking the reservations, cleaning the hotel rooms, and doing other service jobs.

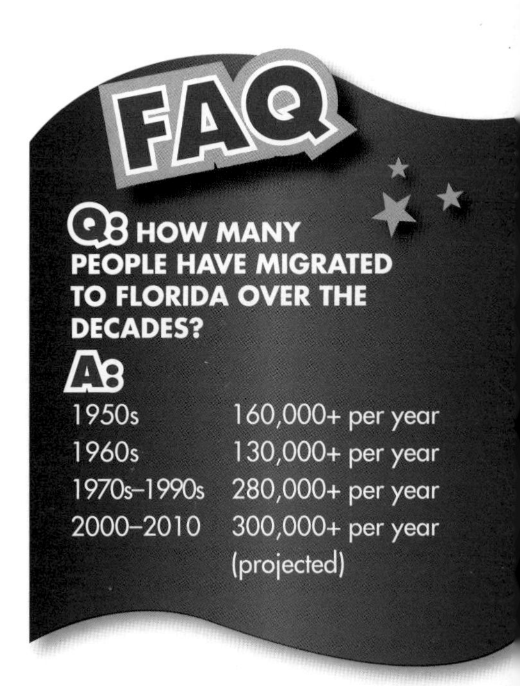

FAQ

Q8 HOW MANY PEOPLE HAVE MIGRATED TO FLORIDA OVER THE DECADES?

A8

1950s	160,000+ per year
1960s	130,000+ per year
1970s–1990s	280,000+ per year
2000–2010	300,000+ per year (projected)

Food in Little Havana has a distinct Cuban flavor.

HOW TO TALK LIKE A FLORIDIAN

There are as many languages as there are ethnic groups in Florida. In Tarpon Springs, you will hear Greek spoken; in Miami, you'll hear Spanish or, in the Jewish neighborhoods, Hebrew. You also might hear French Creole, Portuguese, Chinese, or Polish.

But aside from various languages, Floridians have their own way of saying things. For example:

- "Snowbirds" refers to all of the people who come to Florida during the winter months to escape cold weather.
- "Mosquito hawk" is a dragonfly.
- "Pinder" means peanut.
- "Conch" is the term for people who have lived on one of the Florida Keys for at least seven years.

WOW

Calle Ocho, a free Cuban street festival held each year in Miami, won a mention in the *Guinness Book of World Records* in 1988, when 119,986 people formed the world's longest conga line.

HOW TO EAT LIKE A FLORIDIAN

When you sit down for a meal in Florida, you're in for a treat. The warm climate means that fresh fruits and vegetables are in abundant supply. And the coast provides a daily catch of fish, shrimp, oysters, and other delicious seafood. Florida's multicultural population means you can find dishes with spice! For some examples, see the menu on the opposite page.

A crowd enjoying the Calle Ocho festival

Cuban sandwich

MENU

WHAT'S ON THE MENU IN FLORIDA?

Cuban Sandwich

This sandwich begins with a crusty loaf of bread that is split in half and then piled with layers of ham, pork, Swiss cheese, and pickles. The whole thing is slid into a pizza oven to heat up. Top with a hot peppery sauce, and you're ready to eat!

Fruit

You'll find all kinds of fruit, picked right from the tree. Order a fresh-squeezed juice, or try a fruit kebab—grapes, tangerines, oranges, bananas, and other sweet gems arranged on a long stick.

Seafood

Feast on shrimp, Florida snapper, crab, and a variety of delicacies fresh from the ocean.

Salsa

This sauce (*salsa* is Spanish for "sauce") of chopped tomatoes, onions, cilantro, and other fresh ingredients is the perfect complement to chips, fish, chicken, and other dishes. Some say the spicier, the better!

TRY THIS RECIPE
Key Lime Pie

Florida is known for its citrus, including the round, yellowish green Key lime unique to Key West. The juice of this golf-ball-sized fruit is the main ingredient of Key lime pie, the official pie of the Florida Keys.

Floridians debate the origins of Key lime pie as much as they do what kind of crust it should have. A popular legend has it that William Curry, a ship salvager and one of Florida's first millionaires, had a cook named Sally who invented the pie in the mid-1800s. Nobody thought to write down a recipe until the 1930s. Here is one of the easiest ones (be sure to have a grown-up nearby to help):

Ingredients:

1 14-ounce can sweetened condensed milk
½ cup lime juice
1 graham cracker piecrust
2 cups whipped topping
1 Key lime, sliced into thin rounds for garnish

Instructions:

1. Mix the milk and lime juice together.
2. Pour the mixture into the piecrust.
3. Chill in the refrigerator until set.
4. Top with whipped topping.
5. Garnish the top with lime slices.

Key lime pie

FLORIDA EDUCATION

You can study to be just about anything you want at one of Florida's many universities, colleges, and community colleges. Small colleges include Boca Raton's Digital Media Arts College, where you can learn to do computer animation; the Embry-Riddle Aeronautical University in Daytona Beach, where you can find out about every aspect of flying; the Florida College of Natural Health, which offers courses in acupuncture and massage therapy; and Le Cordon Bleu College of Culinary Arts, where you can learn to be a chef. Florida International University in Miami has more than 38,000 students, and it boasts a great international business program. Florida's largest university is the University of Florida in Gainesville. UF traces its roots to 1853, and today it enrolls more than 50,000 students each year.

Anderson Hall at the University of Florida in Gainesville. This school was founded in 1853.

Willie Reagan (left) Isaac Knight (center), Rodney Demps (right), and Mary Ann Carroll (front) are part of a group of self-taught black artists called the Highwaymen. This group's origins date back to the late 1950s.

To prepare Florida's students for higher education, the Florida Center for Reading Research and the department of education's Just Read, Florida! program are working to promote the value of reading. They give tips for good reading habits for students in elementary through high school and provide resources for parents, teachers, and kids.

ARTS IN THE SUNSHINE STATE

In 1979, a program was developed that featured artwork by state, national, and even international artists in every state building. Since then, the Arts in State Buildings program has purchased or commissioned more than 1,000 works of art to be part of the state's collection. The Arts Learning Gallery in Tallahassee is another place to see rotating exhibitions of art created by local students, as well as professional painters.

THE HIGHWAYMEN

In the late 1950s, a group of 26 African American painters led by Alfred Hair from the Fort Pierce area began painting Florida landscapes. Their teacher was a well-known Florida artist named A. E. "Beanie" Backus. Under his guidance, the young artists produced paintings of sunsets, waterscapes, swamps, and marshes. They loaded their paintings into their cars and traveled along the East Coast selling them, earning themselves the name Highwaymen.

During the 1970s and 1980s, the interest in their art began to fade away. But then, in the 1990s, the Highwaymen's paintings became collectibles. Today, they are highly sought after, and some of them even hang in the governor's executive office.

Want to know more? See www.floridahighwaymen.com

The Vizcaya Museum and Gardens in Miami was once the home of American industrialist John Deering. After his death in 1925, the property was eventually opened to visitors.

The Sunshine State also boasts a number of fine art museums. The Salvador Dalí Museum in Saint Petersburg offers an incredible collection of the 20th century Spaniard's work. And the Vizcaya Museum and Gardens in Miami-Dade County is a National Historic Landmark.

SEE IT HERE!

THE SINGING TOWER

Edward Bok (1863–1930), millionaire and a Pulitzer Prize–winning author, helped to create the 205-foot (62.5-m) Bok Tower—also known as the "singing tower" because of its 57 bells that are played from a keyboard—in Lake Wales. Made out of pink and gray marble and coquina stone, and surrounded by a magnificent garden, it was constructed in the late 1920s.

FLORIDA LITERATURE

A number of classic books have been written in Florida. Writer Ernest Hemingway made his home in Key West, where he wrote some of his best-known works, including *For Whom the Bell Tolls* and *A Farewell to Arms*. And Harlem Renaissance writer and folklorist Zora Neale Hurston spent her childhood in Eatonville. She is remembered for her extraordinary work *Their Eyes Were Watching God*. Marjorie Kinnan Rawlings lived in an orange grove in Hawthorne. She wrote the classic *The Yearling*, about a boy in Florida's swamplands and his adopted fawn.

Other Florida writers include Dave Barry, who is known for his sidesplittingly funny books and newspaper column in the *Miami Herald.* Edward Bloor is a writer and editor who enjoys writing books for young adults. Recent titles include *Story Time, London Calling,* and *Tangerine.* He lives in Winter Park. Tim Dorsey is a Tampa novelist whose crime capers include *The Stingray Shuffle* and *The Big Bamboo.*

MINI-BIO

ZORA NEALE HURSTON: AUTHOR AND ANTHROPOLOGIST

Harlem Renaissance writer Zora Neale Hurston (1891–1960) grew up in Eatonville, the first all-black incorporated town in the United States. After getting a degree in anthropology from Barnard College, Hurston began studying and writing about African American folklore. She also wrote one of the country's most well-known novels, *Their Eyes Were Watching God.*

Later in life, Hurston lived in Fort Pierce and worked in a library in Cape Canaveral. Today, her Fort Pierce home is a National Historic Landmark.

Want to know more? See www.si.umich.edu/chico/harlem/text/hurston.html

Majorie Kinnan Rawlings at work in her Florida home

MINI-BIO

CARL HIAASEN: A FAVORITE AUTHOR

Born in Plantation, Carl Hiaasen (1953–) has spent his life living in and writing about Florida. He started writing for the *Miami Herald* in 1976, and his articles have often focused on controversial environmental issues. In the early 1980s, Hiaasen began writing novels, and his focus was his home state. His books are mostly mystery, with a lot of humor thrown in. He has also written some popular young adult books, including *Hoot* and *Flush*. He and his family live in the Keys.

Want to know more? See www.carlhiaasen.com

ON STAGE AND SCREEN

When you turn on the TV or go see a show, you may just be watching some famous Floridians. Tony Award–winning actor Ben Vereen was born in Miami. He had critically acclaimed roles in numerous Broadway shows and has also appeared in TV shows such as *Roots* and *Star Trek: The Next Generation*. Actor Butterfly McQueen is best remembered for her role as Prissy in *Gone with the Wind*. She was born in Tampa. Actor Sidney Poitier starred in classic films such as *Guess Who's Coming to Dinner*, *Lilies of the Field*, and *In the Heat of the Night*.

Sidney Poitier as Detective Virgil Tibbs in *In the Heat of the Night*, 1967. He won an Academy Award in 1964 for his role in *Lilies of the Field*.

THE MUSIC WORLD

Florida music can have an earthy salsa rhythm, an energizing beat, or a soft ballad sound. The styles of music are as diverse as its people and its history. Singer-songwriter Rob Thomas spent much of his early life in Florida. Formerly of Matchbox Twenty, Thomas is now enjoying a solo career. Boy band *NSYNC originated in Orlando, and rocker Tom Petty was born in Gainesville. Longtime Key West resident Jimmy Buffett is a writer and musician. His devoted fans are known as "parrotheads." Criteria Studios in Miami has produced songs by many well-known artists, such as Bob Dylan and 10,000 Maniacs.

MINI-BIO

GLORIA ESTEFAN: THE VOICE FROM HAVANA

Born in Havana, Cuba, Gloria Estefan (1957–) spent most of her childhood in Miami. In the mid-1980s, she hit the radio waves with the dance hits she performed with her group, The Miami Sound Machine. She married the band's keyboardist. In 1988, the group was renamed Gloria Estefan and the Miami Sound Machine, but by the end of the decade, it was just Gloria Estefan. After a serious auto accident, Estefan took a year off, but she was back on the charts in 1991. In the 21st century, the Grammy Award–winning artist has returned to her Latina roots by producing all-Spanish albums.

Want to know more? See www.gloriaestefan.com

GOOD SPORTS

The great weather in Florida makes it the perfect place to play sports. Florida boasts dozens of golf courses that host a number of professional tournaments. Among them are the Doral Golf Resort in Miami and the Bay Hill Club in Orlando. Florida is also home to the famous Nick Bollettieri Tennis Academy. Located in Bradenton, this school has taught tennis greats such as Pete Sampras, Maria Sharapova, Andre Agassi, Jim Courier, and Martina Hingis. Chris Evert is a native Floridian who was the number-one female player in the world during the 1970s. She passes her love of the game on to students at the Evert Tennis Academy in Boca Raton.

MINI-BIO

DAVID ROBINSON: THE ADMIRAL

When he enrolled in the U.S. Naval Academy, David Robinson (1965–) was already 6'4" (193 cm). By the time he graduated, however, he was *really* tall! He was 7'1" (216 cm)! Three years later, he was an All-American center and college basketball player of the year. Then he was drafted by the professional San Antonio Spurs and was named rookie of the year. Nicknamed "The Admiral," Robinson led the NBA in rebounds, blocked shots, and scoring. He retired after the 2002–2003 season. The only male player to play on three Olympic teams (1988, 1992, and 1996), Robinson was born in Key West.

There are lots of sports to watch, too. Many major league baseball teams have spring training in the Sunshine State. Come late winter, you'll find the New York Yankees in Tampa, the New York Mets in Port St. Lucie, the St. Louis Cardinals in Jupiter, and the Philadelphia Phillies in Clearwater—just to name a few. And two baseball teams make Florida their home year-round: the Florida Marlins of Miami and the Tampa Bay Devil Rays.

Floridians love football, too. The Miami Dolphins have been wowing NFL fans for years. And many Florida colleges have powerhouse football teams. They include the Florida State Seminoles and the University of Florida Gators. The Gators won the 2006 national championship.

If basketball is your game, you'll enjoy watching the Orlando Magic and the Miami Heat. The Heat captured the NBA championship in 2006. Speaking of hoops, the University of Florida Gators men's basketball team clinched back-to-back NCAA championships in 2006 and 2007. Their defeat of the Ohio State Buckeyes for the 2007 championship came just months after the Gators football squad defeated the Buckeyes in the Bowl Championship Series national title game. The school became the only program in history to hold both championships at the same time. Go Gators!

Coach Billy Donovan celebrates with the Florida Gators after winning the 2007 NCAA men's basketball championship.

A GREAT PLACE TO BE

No matter what your interest—sports, music, literature, terrific food, or amazing art—you can find it in Florida. With its richly diverse population, thriving cultural scene, great schools, and pleasant climate, Florida is a wonderful place to live.

READ ABOUT

A sculpture of dolphins at the State Capitol in Tallahassee

GOVERNMENT

★

FLORIDA'S GOVERNMENT IS RUN BY SOME OF THE STATE'S MOST CREATIVE, HARDWORKING, AND DEDICATED PEOPLE. They must be, in order to deal with some of the most complicated issues in the nation. If there's a bad winter, they have to figure out how to help the farmers who have lost important citrus crops. In the event of a devastating hurricane, they need to make plans for evacuation in advance and disaster relief in the aftermath. The tourism industry depends on the state's beautiful environment, and it's up to the government to protect the land from becoming overdeveloped.

SEAT OF GOVERNMENT

In 1823, two explorers set out to find a central location for their territory's government. One came from St. Augustine and the other came from Pensacola. They met in the middle in a beautiful place the Seminole called Tallahassee, meaning "old town." Since it was about halfway between the two big cities, it was declared the new capital.

Today, Tallahassee is a fast-growing area and is home to both Florida State University and Florida A&M University. Behind the capitol is a seven-block section of Adam Street that is now a pedestrian mall. It includes a government plaza with buildings such as city hall, the county courthouse, and the governor's mansion.

The old capitol now houses a museum. In the background is the new capitol, which was dedicated in 1978.

SEE IT HERE!

THE OLD CAPITOL

Florida's first capitol was a set of three log cabins in Tallahassee. In 1839, Congress gave Florida $20,000 for the construction of a new capitol. The original one was torn down and replaced with a brick model in 1845. In 1902, a dome was added. It was the government's home until 1972, when the legislature provided the funds for a new capitol. In 1978, all the employees left the old capitol to go to the new one. Four years later, the old capitol was opened as the Museum of Florida History.

Capitol Facts

Here are some fascinating facts about Florida's state capitol.

It was built using:

- 3,700 tons of structural steel
- 2,800 tons of reinforcing steel
- 25,000 cubic yards of concrete (19,000 cu m)—equal to 16 football fields

Inside it includes:

- 12,000 square feet (1,100 sq m) of walnut paneling
- 12,000 gallons (45,400 liters) of paint
- 62,000 square feet (5,800 sq m) of marble
- 60,000 square feet (5,600 sq m) of carpet
- 30 miles (48 km) of telephone cable
- 250 miles (402 km) of electrical cable

The building is 718,000 square feet (66,700 sq m), and it took 1,016 days to build.

Capital City

This map shows places of interest in Tallahassee, Florida's capital city.

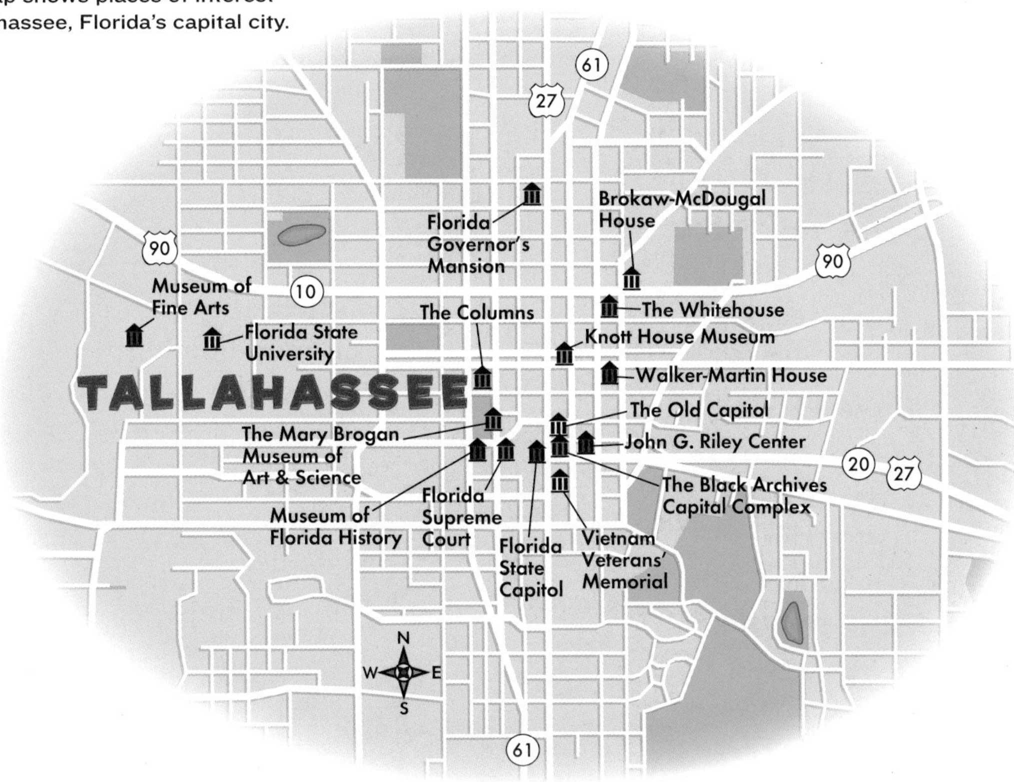

The Florida house of representatives in session. Its 120 members help pass laws for the state.

MINI-BIO

WILLIAM DUNN MOSELEY: FIRST GOVERNOR OF FLORIDA

Born in North Carolina, William Dunn Moseley (1795–1863) served in the North Carolina senate for eight years. In 1835, he bought a plantation and moved to Lake Miccosukee. Florida was not yet a state, so Moseley served in the territorial house of representatives and then the territorial senate. After Florida became a state in 1845, Moseley was elected the first governor. While in office, he oversaw the state's role in the Mexican-American War (1846–1848) and tried to settle disputes with the Seminole people. Moseley was a strong supporter of state-funded public schools.

Two years after serving a single term as governor, Moseley settled in the town of Palatka and operated a citrus grove.

THE EXECUTIVE BRANCH

Just like the other states, Florida has a government with three distinct branches: the executive, the legislative, and the judicial. The governor is in charge of the executive branch. He or she is elected to a four-year term and can serve only two terms in a row. The governor runs the executive branch with the help and guidance of the lieutenant governor. The governor is also advised by the secretary of state, attorney general, and several committees. This is the branch that puts the laws into action.

One governor who worked to help Florida grow was C. Farris Bryant. Elected in 1960, he helped secure funds for creating state junior colleges and universities. He encouraged the building of interstate and state highways in Florida. And he made sure to purchase public lands for future use by the state. His efforts helped Florida prosper.

Only two Florida governors have served two full four-year terms: Reuben Askew (1971–1979) and Jeb Bush (1999–2007).

Florida State Government

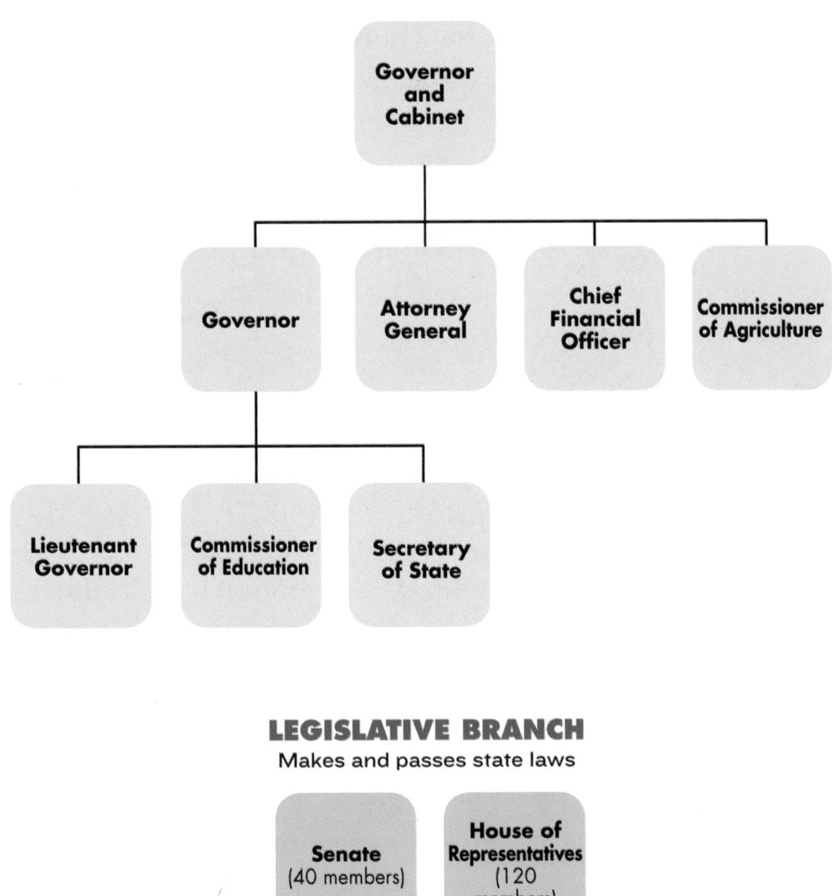

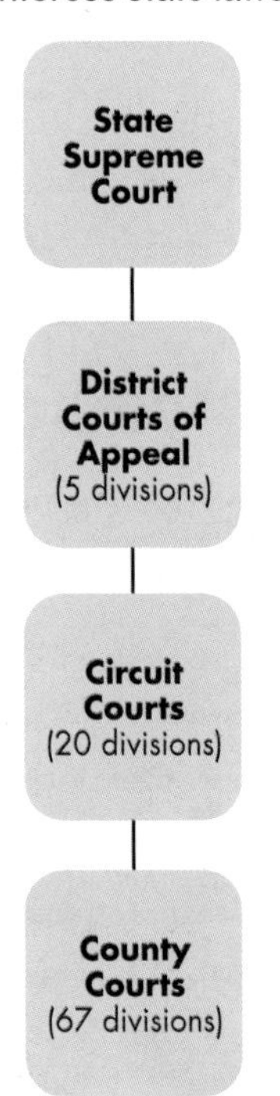

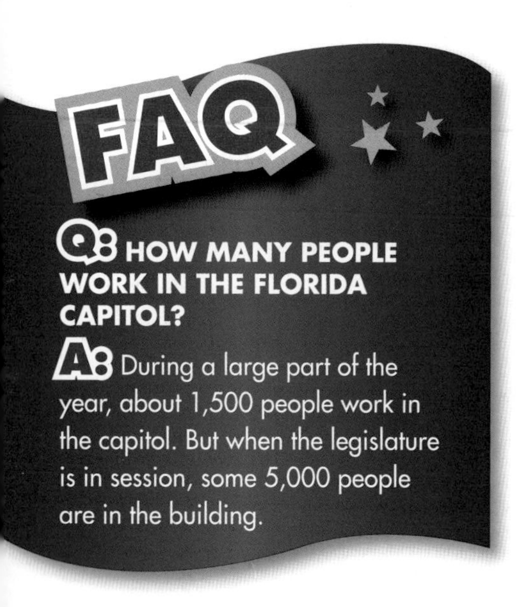

FAQ
Q HOW MANY PEOPLE WORK IN THE FLORIDA CAPITOL?
A During a large part of the year, about 1,500 people work in the capitol. But when the legislature is in session, some 5,000 people are in the building.

THE LEGISLATIVE BRANCH

The legislative branch is divided into two houses: the Senate, which has 40 members, and the House of Representatives, which has 120 members. Their jobs are to create and pass laws. Some of those laws regulate the need for seat belts and child safety seats in cars, how old you have to be to get a driver's license, where people can and can't smoke, and what materials must be recycled.

Dozens of Florida state legislators have served with distinction, including Mary Grizzle. A representative for 15 years, Grizzle served in the senate from 1978 to 1990. During her career in public service, she helped pass laws to restrict sewage being dumped into Tampa Bay. She also helped set standards for clean water. She was never afraid to lead a fight, and during her life, the environment and women's rights were among her favorite causes. As former senator Curtis Kiser remembers, "Mary was ahead of her time. She just stood her ground. She was just a tiger."

Representing Florida

This list shows the number of elected officials who represent Florida, both on the state and national levels.

OFFICE	NUMBER	LENGTH OF TERM
State senators	40	4 years
State representatives	120	2 years
U.S. senators	2	6 years
U.S. representatives	25	2 years
Presidential electors	25	—

THE JUDICIAL BRANCH

The judicial branch is made up of judges and courts. They are the ones who look at the facts, figure out the law, and then make a ruling in the court. Judges help people settle family and neighborhood disputes. They also oversee trials for serious crimes. Like other states, Florida has multiple levels of courts, from the state supreme court to the lower courts. The smallest problems are taken care of in city courts.

Florida Counties

This map shows the 67 counties in Florida. Tallahassee, the state capital, is indicated with a star.

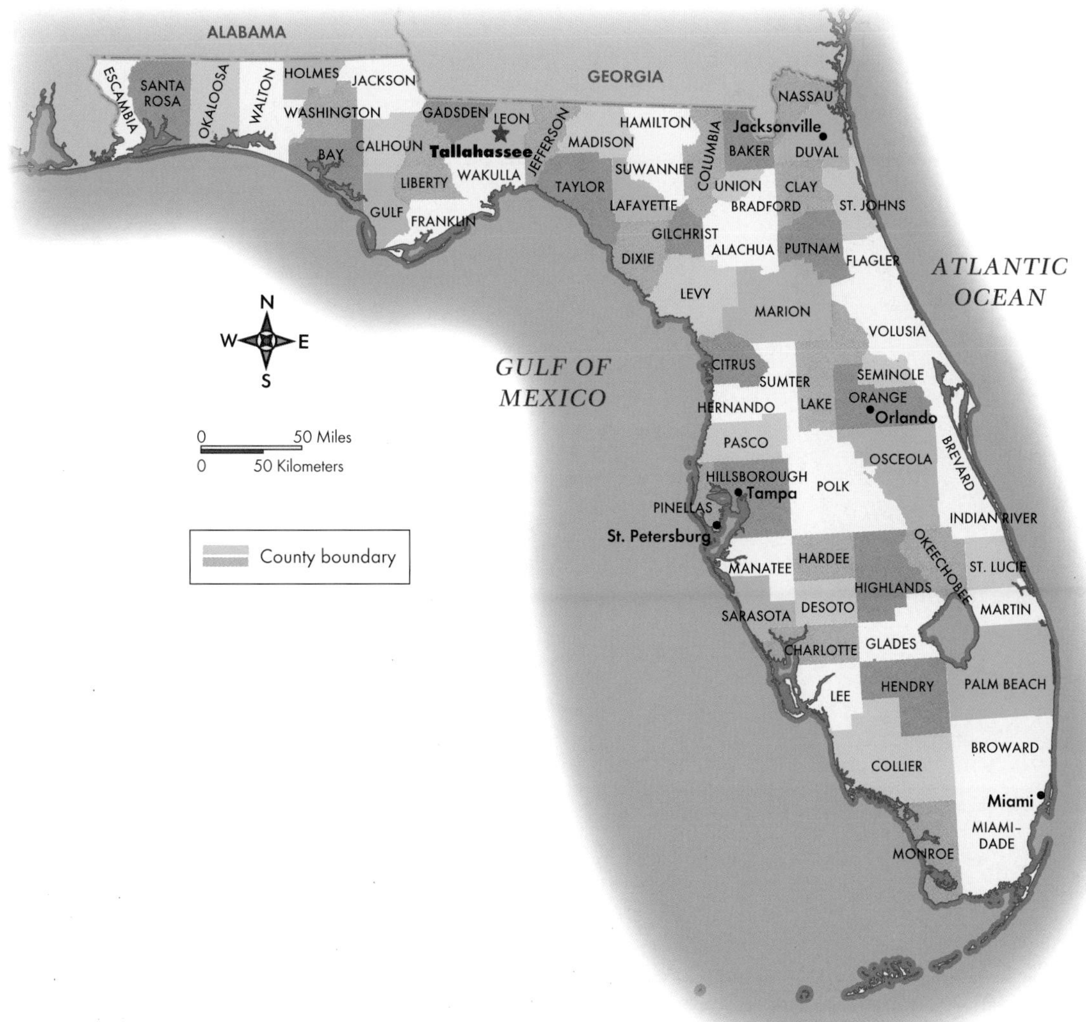

LOCAL GOVERNMENT

Along with Florida's state government, there is also a system of county governments. The state has 67 counties and 405 municipalities, or incorporated cities. Each county elects officials such as a county auditor, clerk, coroner, district attorney, sheriff, school superintendent, and treasurer.

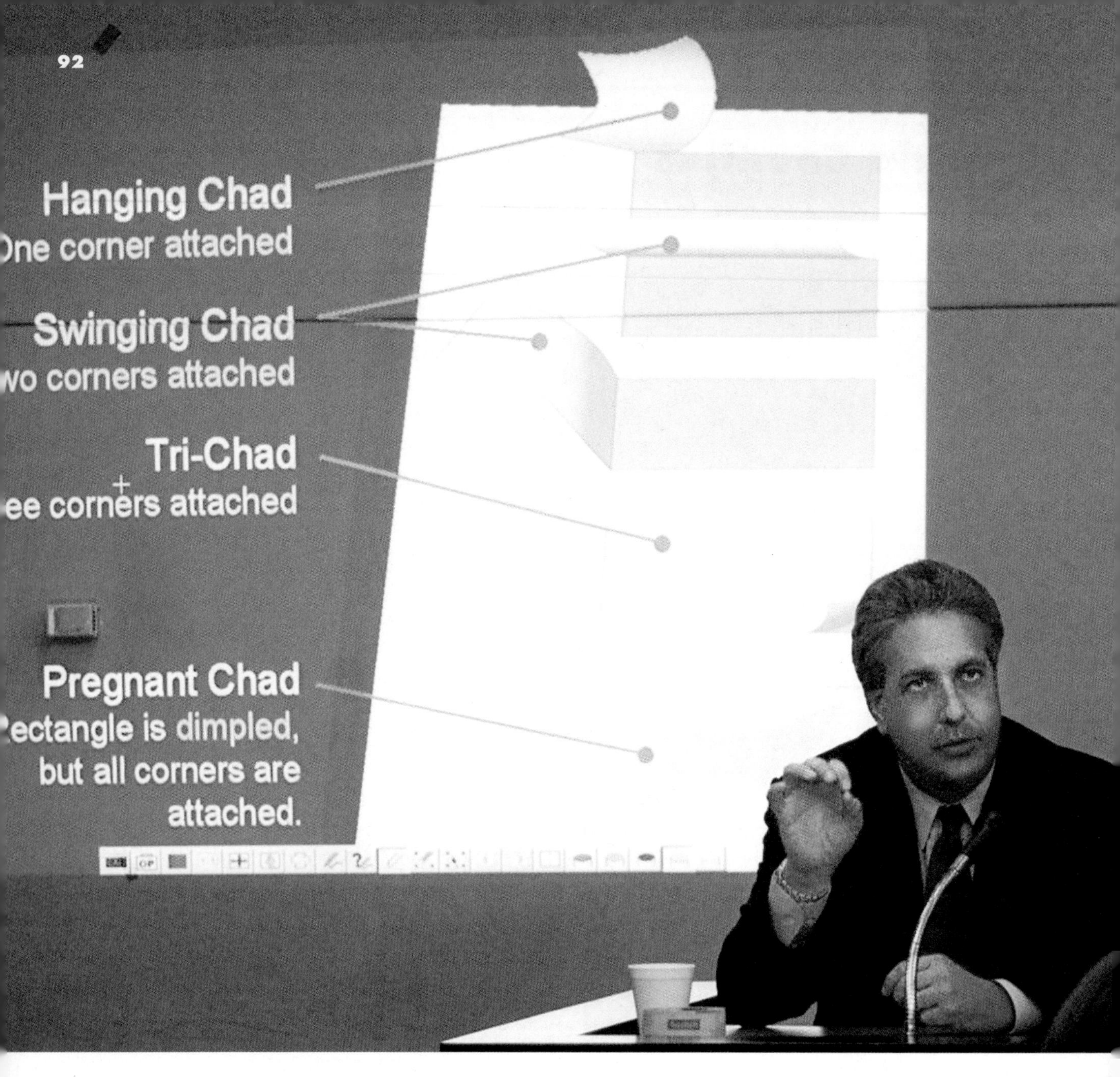

For weeks after the 2000 presidential election, officials tried to sort out allegations of miscounted votes. Here, Judge Charles Burton of Palm Beach County testifies. And the visual exhibit illustrates chads, the holes that are punched through paper ballots.

Sometimes local government gets national attention. In the 2000 presidential election, the race between George W. Bush and Al Gore was very close. And some voters in Florida claimed that the ballots were misleading and their votes were being counted wrong. There was a huge debate about this issue. So Florida votes had to be counted and recounted. This took weeks! Finally, the U.S. Supreme Court halted the recount and the election was awarded to George W. Bush, who became the next U.S. president.

SEEING HOW LAWMAKERS WORK

To encourage Florida's young people to participate in government, each year the Senate invites students between the ages of 15 and 18 to Tallahassee to work as pages and messengers for one week. The same kind of program exists in the U.S. House of Representatives, as well. These pages (between ages 12 and 14) and messengers (between ages 15 and 18) get a behind-the-scenes look at Florida government while they hand out materials and deliver messages to senators and their staff. Who knows—they may be tomorrow's lawmakers!

MINI-BIO

ILEANA ROS-LEHTINEN: FLORIDA REPRESENTATIVE

Born in Cuba, Ileana Ros-Lehtinen (1952–) moved to Florida when she was seven years old. She attended Florida International University and founded Eastern Academy, a private elementary school. In 1982, she turned from education to politics and was elected to the Florida House of Representatives. After serving a term, Ros-Lehtinen became a state senator. In 1988, she was elected to the U.S. House of Representatives, the first Hispanic woman to serve in Congress. She served on the Foreign Affairs Committee, and she played a key role in the discussion of the Cuban Democracy Act, which prohibits U.S. corporations from trading with Cuba.

Want to know more? See www.house.gov/ros-lehtinen

WEIRD AND WACKY LAWS

In Florida, the state legislature works hard to keep the laws relevant and helpful—so hard that they haven't had a chance yet to strike these from the books:

- It is illegal to sing in public while wearing a swimsuit.
- Unmarried women are not allowed to parachute on Sunday.
- If an elephant is tied to a parking meter, a parking fee has to be paid, just as for a vehicle.

State Flag

Adopted in 1900, Florida's official flag features a red cross of Saint Andrew on a white field. In the center is the state seal. Between 1868 and 1900, Florida's state flag consisted of a white field with the state seal in the center. During the late 1890s, Governor Francis P. Fleming suggested that a red cross be added, so that the banner did not appear to be a white flag of truce or surrender when hanging still on a flagpole.

State Seal

The Florida state seal was first created in 1868. The original specifications called for the seal to include the sun's rays, a cocoa tree, a steamboat, and a Native American woman scattering flowers. These images were to be circled by the words, "Great Seal of the State of Florida: In God We Trust."

In the years since, several updates have been made. Designers removed the woman's feathered headdress (only male Seminoles wore headdresses), so she is now a more authentic Seminole. They flattened a mountain in the background (since Florida has no mountains), and replaced the original cocoa tree with a sabal palm to reflect its adoption as the official state tree in 1953.

READ ABOUT

"Partners"
"We believe in our idea: a family park where parents and children could have fun - together."

Walt Disney World employs thousands of service workers who help take care of visitors to the park each day.

ECONOMY

★

WHEN YOU THINK OF FLORIDA'S ECONOMY, YOU MIGHT JUST PICTURE ORANGES. Florida grows oranges—it's true—and a variety of other crops. But agriculture isn't its only business. Florida's miles of coastline and nearness to Latin America make it an ideal place for international trade. A whopping 40 percent of everything the United States exports to its southern neighbors passes through Florida. With 86 million visitors a year, Florida has one of the world's top tourism industries. Florida is more than oranges!

CONCENTRATE!

During World War II, the federal government turned to the Florida Citrus Commission for help. The soldiers in the battlefield were desperate for vitamin C. At the time, there was a powdered form of OJ and a thick, syrupy version, but neither was very tasty.

For three years, C. D. Atkins, Louis MacDowell, and Edwin Moore worked in a small lab in Winter Haven. They finally figured out how to make a **concentrate** of the juice and freeze it. But by the time the patent came through, the war was over. So the new product was used commercially. Check the orange juice in your refrigerator. Is the juice made from concentrate?

Harvesting strawberries in a Florida field

WORD TO KNOW

concentrate *a food that has excess water removed from it*

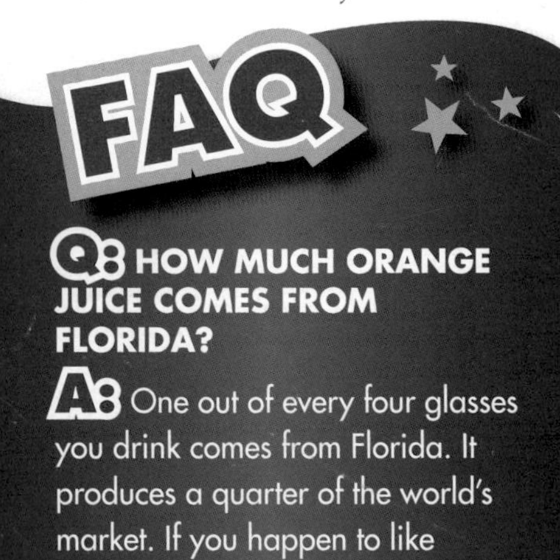

Q: HOW MUCH ORANGE JUICE COMES FROM FLORIDA?

A: One out of every four glasses you drink comes from Florida. It produces a quarter of the world's market. If you happen to like grapefruit juice, two out of every four glasses began in Florida.

ORCHARDS AND FIELDS

Why do fruits and vegetables grow so well in Florida? It's the warm temperature and plentiful rain combined with rich soil that makes it ideal for agriculture. Farming is an important part of the state economy. There are about 44,000 farms throughout Florida, and each one averages about 300 acres (120 ha). Although it may seem like citrus fruit is the only produce to come out of Florida, there is more. The state is actually second only to California for its production of green peppers, cucumbers, celery, and potatoes. Growers in the Everglades provide a great deal of sugarcane. The central and southeastern parts of the state produce dairy products and beef cattle.

Top Products

Manufacturing	computer and electronic products, food and beverage processing, transportation equipment
Agriculture	oranges, other citrus, tomatoes, sugarcane, livestock/livestock products
Mining	phosphate rock, crushed stone

What Do Floridians Do?

This color-coded chart shows what industries Floridians work in.

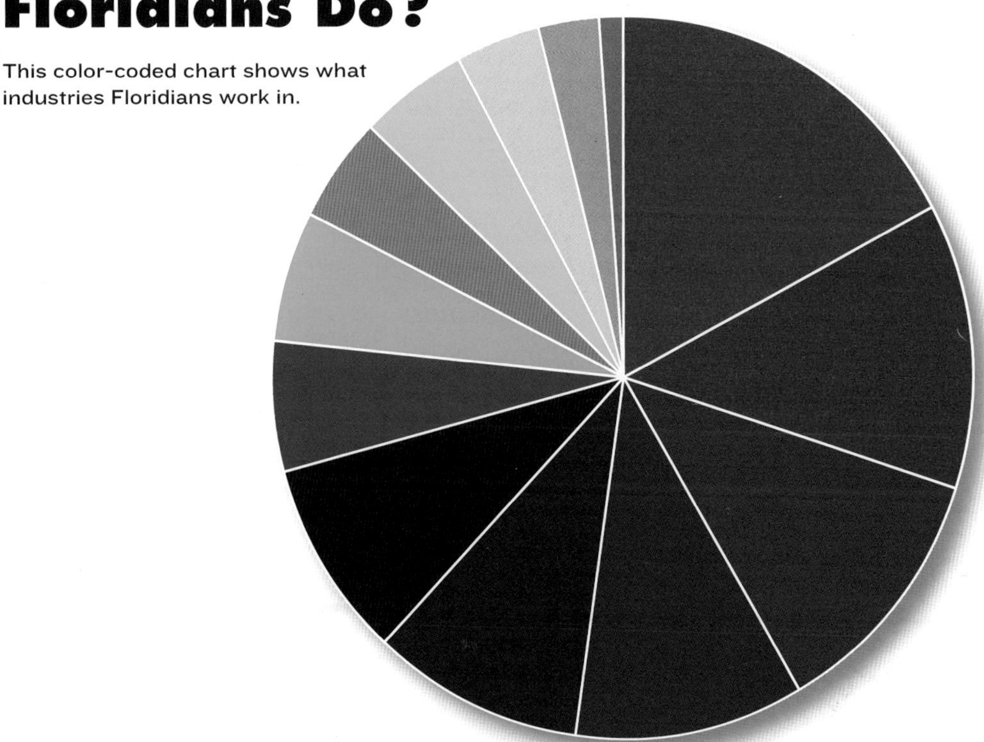

18.2% Educational, health and social services, 1,436,783

12.8% Retail trade, 1,006,750

11.4% Professional, scientific, management, administrative, and waste management services, 900,695

10.4% Arts, entertainment, recreation, accommodation and food services, 824,239

10.2% Construction, 804,994

8.7% Finance, insurance, real estate, and rental and leasing, 685,107

6.2% Manufacturing, 488,255

5.1% Transportation and warehousing, and utilities, 401,970

5.0% Other services (except public administration), 396,044

4.8% Public administration, 374,736

3.8% Wholesale trade, 302,731

2.4% Information, 193,328

1.0% Agriculture, forestry, fishing and hunting, and mining, 81,018

Source: U.S. Census Bureau, 2005

THE EARTH AND SEA

Florida's land is rich with minerals. The state's leading mining product is phosphate rock, which is used in fertilizer. It is mainly found in Polk County. Florida also produces masonry cement and crushed stones that are used in construction.

Each day, Florida fishers head out into area waters. Their catches include shrimp, crab, fish, and lobster. Most of these end up in local seafood restaurants and supermarkets.

The shrimping industry alone is huge, bringing in $185 million to the state each year. Aquaculture, which includes the business of tropical fish, aquatic plants, harvesting clams, and catching fish, is responsible for some $1.3 billion a year for Florida's economy.

A fisher in Jupiter Inlet, north Palm Beach, with a net full of fish

Major Agricultural and Mining Products

This map shows where Florida's major agricultural and mining products come from. See a pick and shovel? That means minerals are found there.

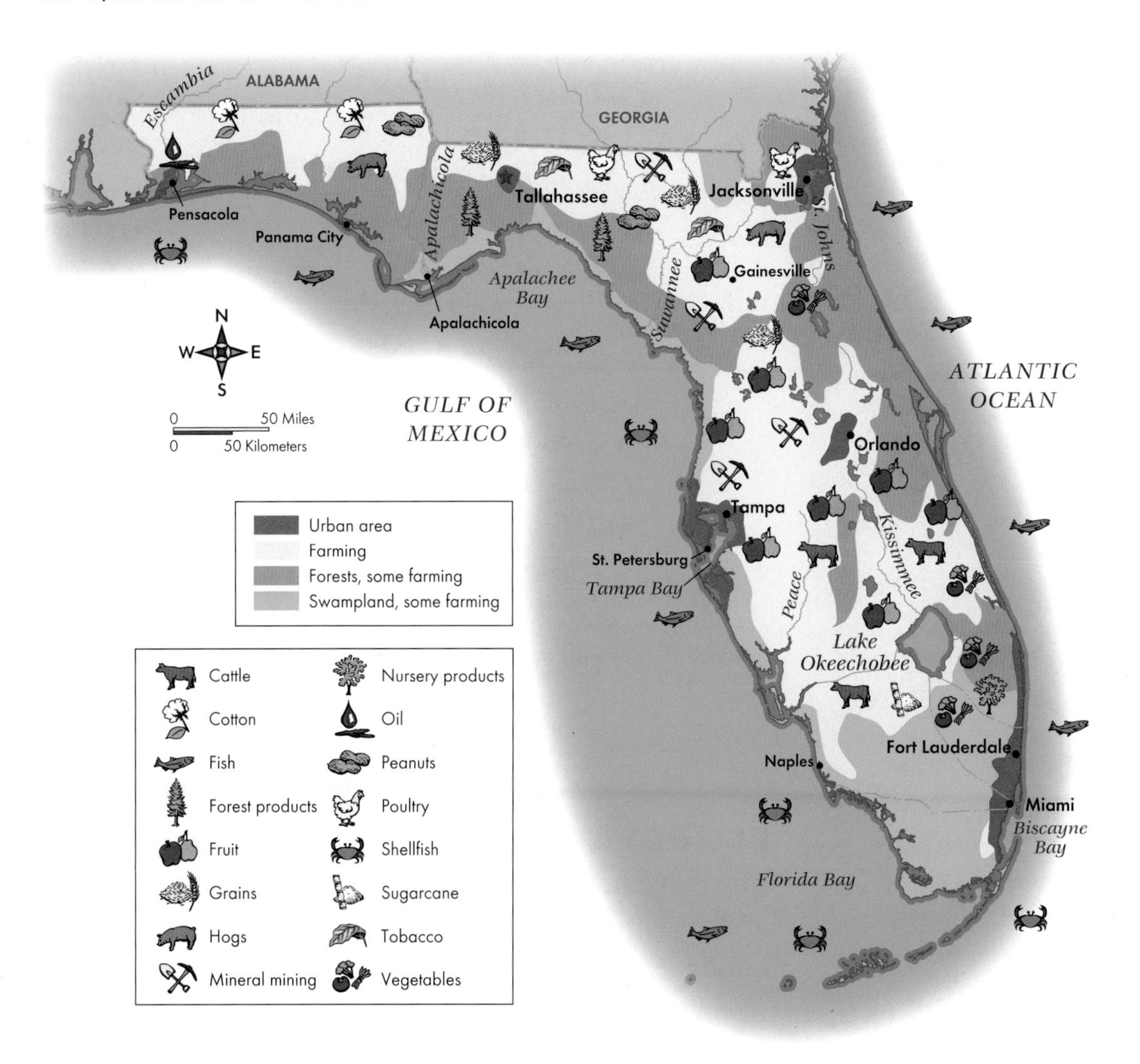

ALAMEDA FREE LIBRARY

A BAD FISHING TRIP—A GREAT OPPORTUNITY

He only meant to catch a few fish, but he ended up catching a great idea instead. When George Goodwin went fishing in the early 1970s, he kept snagging his lures on logs instead of fish. The logs he snagged with his hook were deadhead logs. These are logs that were supposed to have floated downstream to the mill a century before. But because they were so full of **resin**, they sank instead.

This wood going to waste at the bottom of the riverbed intrigued Goodwin. He discovered that even though the exterior of the wood rots while underwater, the inside is preserved. When milled, the interior makes beautiful flooring and paneling.

Goodwin took every penny he had and bought 20 acres (8 ha) of land and put an old sawmill on the property. Then he and his wife paid divers to bring up the logs from the water. The logs were cleaned up and sold. In 1977, Goodwin Heart Pine made $5,000. In 2004, it made $3 million. That fishing trip was a successful one indeed.

WORD TO KNOW

resin *clear or light-colored material that is secreted by trees and other plants; used in varnishes, printing inks, and other products*

WALLACE AMOS JR.: COOKIE KING

If you like chocolate chip cookies, you most likely recognize the name Famous Amos. He is known as the man whose "face launched a thousand chips." He was born Wallace Amos Jr. (1936–) in Tallahassee and moved to New York City when he was 12 years old. He spent four years in the U.S. Air Force and, in 1962, became the first African American talent agent in the history of the William Morris Agency.

In 1967, he left the agency and struck out on his own. He tried several businesses, but finally started baking cookies as his aunt had once done for him when he was young. They were a hit! The first cookie store opened in 1975, and a few months later, he opened two more stores. For the next decade, Amos built a cookie empire. In 1998, Keebler Foods Company purchased the brand.

FLORIDA FACTORIES

The Sunshine State is not only home to Cape Canaveral and the Kennedy Space Center, but many defense and scientific research companies have headquarters in Florida. At NASA, the Environmental Research Aircraft and Sensor Technology program focuses on developing full-size planes that do not need pilots. In the same building, scientists make tools and instruments for remote-controlled aircraft. Major air and naval facilities can be found near the cities of Tampa and Pensacola. With attractions such

Characters from Davy Crockett's Tall Tales, an amusement ride located in Texas but created by Sally Corporation in Jacksonville

as Walt Disney World and Universal Studios theme park, the drive to build better robots and **animatronics** has spurred many new businesses, as well. Sally Corporation in Jacksonville is one of the world's premier designers of animatronics and thrill rides.

WORD TO KNOW

animatronics *puppets or other figures that are designed in an electronic way*

THE SERVICE INDUSTRY

Over the years, Florida has become a great vacation spot. The state offers hundreds of hotels, restaurants, museums, and theme parks to keep visitors happy. Service workers—clerks and cooks, tour guides and ticket sellers, even the person in the Mickey Mouse costume—wait on tourists every day. But Florida offers other services, as well. Doctors and nurses care for Florida residents and visitors. Bankers help people save money and borrow money to buy houses and cars. Repair workers fix broken appliances and automobiles.

Despite the hurricanes that tore through the area in 2004 and 2005, Florida's economy has bounced back and is going strong. It leads the nation in new job growth and is attracting more tourists than ever. Nothing seems to slow Florida down.

SEE IT HERE!

THRILL RIDES

Sally Corporation in Jacksonville offers tours that reveal how its employees design and build robots and thrill rides for theme parks around the world. See for yourself how rides come to life!

A bank in Miami installed an ATM designed especially for in-line skaters.

Interstate highway
95
65
ALABAMA
GEORGIA
75
ATLANTIC
OCEAN
DeFuniak Springs
10
Marianna
Valparaiso
Grayton Beach
Fort Walton
Pensacola
Panama City Beach
Panama City
Apalachicola
Apalachicola
Tallahassee
Jacksonville
Olustee
St. Johns
St. Augustine
Suwannee
Gainesville
Ormand Beach
Daytona Beach
Port Orange
Ponce Inlet
Ocala
Sanford
Titusville
Orlando
Kissimmee
Cape Canaveral
Spring Hill
GULF OF
MEXICO
Tarpon Springs
4
Melbourne
Winter Haven
Tampa
Lakeland
Palm Bay
Clearwater
Brandon
Kissimmee
Vero Beach
St. Petersburg
Fort Pierce
Tampa Bay
Bradenton
Port St. Luci
Sarasota
Hobe
Sound
Port Charlotte
Lake
Okeechobee
West
Palm
Beach
Fort Myers
Fort
Lauderdale
Naples
Miami
Beach
Everglades City
Miami
N
W
E
S
0
50 Miles
0
50 Kilometers
Key Largo
Key West
FLORIDA KEYS

CHAPTER NINE

TRAVEL GUIDE

TRAVEL GUIDE

★

NOW THAT YOU'VE READ ALL ABOUT FLORIDA'S GEOGRAPHY, HISTORY, AND CULTURE, YOU ARE PROBABLY READY TO SEE IT FOR YOURSELF. Begin with a visit to Tallahassee, where you can tour the state capitol or visit the lush pinelands and saw grass plains of the Everglades. If it's action you want, head over to the Daytona International Speedway for an exciting car race, or enjoy the thrills at Universal Studios! What are you waiting for? Grab your map, and let's go!

← Follow along with this travel map. We'll begin in Pensacola and travel all the way south to Key West!

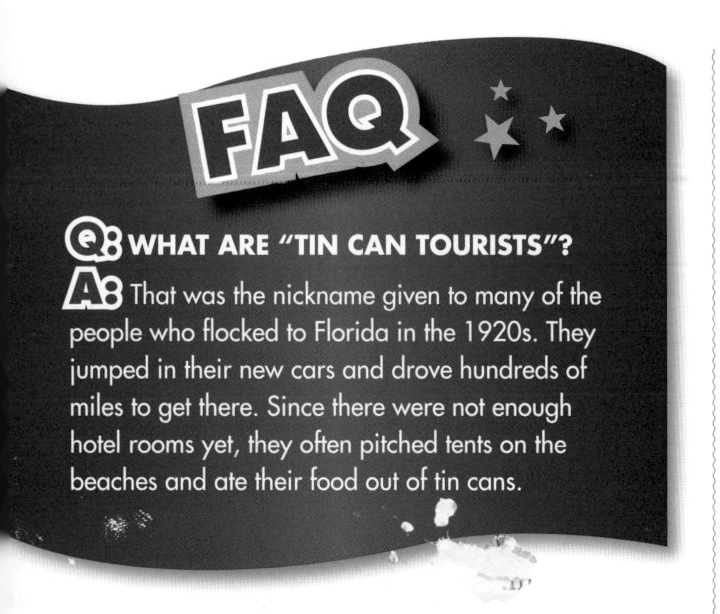

Q: WHAT ARE "TIN CAN TOURISTS"?

A: That was the nickname given to many of the people who flocked to Florida in the 1920s. They jumped in their new cars and drove hundreds of miles to get there. Since there were not enough hotel rooms yet, they often pitched tents on the beaches and ate their food out of tin cans.

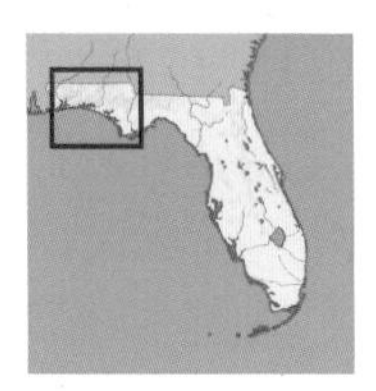

NORTHWEST

THINGS TO DO: Take a bead-making class at the Belmont Arts and Cultural Center, view the treasures at the Heritage Museum of Northwest Florida, or get completely lost in a human maze!

Pensacola

★ **Belmont Arts and Cultural Center:** This working arts center houses the only public glassblowing gallery in the state of Florida. There are even belly dancing classes! At Family Art Days, you can learn glassblowing, pottery, or bead making in just a few hours.

Fort Walton Beach

★ **Sam's Fun City:** From laser tag to bumper cars and waterslides, Sam's Fun City is a place to let loose and have some fun!

Valparaiso

★ **Heritage Museum of Northwest Florida:** At this museum, you'll find artifacts, photographs, and documents pertaining to the history of Northwest Florida, as well as Native American artifacts, the Crestview train station, and pioneer tools.

Fort Walton

★ **Fort Walton Beach:** Pack your sunscreen, flip-flops, beach towel, and a good book for a day at Fort Walton Beach.

DeFuniak Springs

★ **Lake DeFuniak:** A geological treasure, Lake DeFuniak is almost perfectly round! As you stroll along the perimeter of the lake, Victorian residences line its shores.

★ **Walton-DeFuniak Library:** This is the oldest library in Florida still serving the public. Its holdings include a priceless collection of medieval weaponry.

Fishing at Lake DeFuniak

Grayton Beach

★ **Grayton Beach State Park:** Surf's up! Grayton Beach is considered one of America's most beautiful beaches. Visitors can canoe or kayak on Western Lake, hike a trail through coastal forest, or simply sunbathe.

Panama City

★ **Coconut Creek Family Fun Park:** Hit the links at Coconut Creek's two 18-hole mini-golf courses, or get lost in the Gran Maze, which is about the size of a football field!

★ **Junior Museum—The Adventure Place:** Visit this hands-on science and history museum, complete with a Body Works exhibit and hands-on science lab rooms.

Panama City Beach

★ **Shipwreck Island Waterpark:** This is a tropical oasis on Panama City Beach. A wave pool, children's area, Lazy River, giant waterslides, and more provide a fantastic day of family fun.

Marianna

★ **Florida Caverns State Park:** This park has the only walk-through caves in the state. Learn to identify soda straws, flowstones, draperies, and other dazzling formations on one of the daily cave tours.

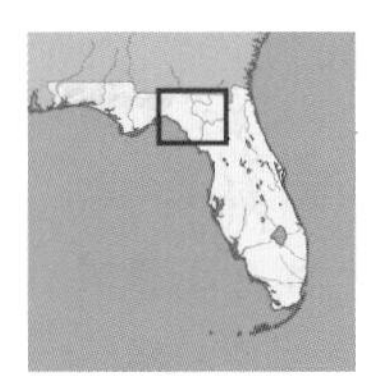

NORTH CENTRAL

THINGS TO DO: Learn about the state's past at the Museum of Florida History, and be sure to visit the Florida State Capitol.

Tallahassee

★ **Museum of Florida History:** Here you'll find exhibits, educational programs, and artifacts that explore and explain Florida's past and present cultures.

★ **Challenger Learning Center of Tallahassee:** Are math and science your thing? Then this museum is for you. With hands-on simulators, immersive theaters, a Space Mission Simulator, an IMAX theater and a high-def full-dome Digistar 3 digital planetarium, this is a must-visit for techies!

★ **Mission San Luis:** Explore Florida's past through living history exhibits, re-created period buildings, and archaeological excavations at the only reconstructed Spanish mission in Florida.

★ **Tallahassee Automobile Museum:** Gearheads beware! The Tallahassee Automobile Museum offers a glimpse at more than 80 rare antique automobiles that auto aficionados will surely appreciate!

★ **Florida State Capitol:** Visit the house and senate legislative building, where some of Florida's most important decisions are discussed, debated, and decided.

Mandrill at the Jacksonville Zoo

NORTHEAST

THINGS TO DO: Visit amazing animals, take a trip back in time, or explore the geological history of the state.

Jacksonville

★ **Jacksonville Zoo and Gardens:** Featuring the only walking safari in northeast Florida, you can see more than 1,500 rare and unusual animal species, as well as more than 1,500 unique plant species!

★ **Museum of Science and History:** Be sure you've got plenty of time to experience 12,000 years of history in the Currents of Time exhibit. You can also see snakes, turtles, birds, owls, baby alligators, and other native creatures in the Florida Naturalist's Center.

★ **Museum of Contemporary Art Jacksonville:** This is the largest modern and contemporary art museum in the southeast region of the country. Check out the Art Walk around Jacksonville, summer film series, and weekend art-making activities.

★ **Jacksonville Jaguars at Alltel Stadium:** Head for the stadium to cheer on the hometown Jacksonville Jaguars, the city's professional football team.

St. Augustine

★ **Colonial Spanish Quarter:** This living history museum explores the world of the early Spanish colonists —with the help of actors! You can visit soldiers and their families and learn about their daily lives. You'll also meet various craftspeople, such as a candle maker, leather-worker, herbalist, blacksmith, and carpenter.

St. Augustine City Hall

★ **The Oldest Wooden Schoolhouse in the USA:** The professor invites you into his classroom to teach you what school life was like more than 200 years ago. Compare your school days with those of the old days. The wooden building is one of St. Augustine's oldest surviving structures.

★ **Mission of Nombre de Dios:** Florida history surrounds you at this mission, which traces its roots to the 1565 founding of St. Augustine.

Gainesville

★ **Florida Museum of Natural History:** In the Hall of Florida Fossils, visitors learn about Florida's fossils and geologic and environmental changes over 65 million years. The South Florida People & Environments exhibit explains the story of Native people in South Florida.

★ **Hippodrome State Theatre:** Here you can see the work of award-winning playwrights, designers, directors, and actors. Recent shows include *Dracula*, *A Christmas Carol*, and *The War of the Worlds*.

Museum of Science and Industry

WEST CENTRAL

THINGS TO DO: Experience life under the sea, hike with dinosaurs, or view some great art.

Tampa

★ **MOSI—Museum of Science and Industry:** At this amazing place, you can get blown away in a Gulf Coast hurricane. Or cruise the galaxy in the Saunders Planetarium. Try strolling through the BioWorks Butterfly Garden or pedaling a high-wire bike three stories above the MOSI grand lobby!

★ **The Florida Aquarium:** Here you'll see more than 10,000 aquatic plants and animals, from huge sharks to playful river otters. There are behind-the-scenes tours, dive shows, close-up animal encounters, and two touch-tanks for hands-on experiences.

★ **Dinosaur World:** See more than 150 life-sized dinosaurs in an outdoor museum setting. Search for authentic fossils to take home at the fossil dig, visit an indoor dinosaur museum, or uncover bones at the Boneyard.

SEE IT HERE!

THE WINTER STRAWBERRY CAPITAL OF THE WORLD

Do you love strawberries? Head for the Winter Strawberry Capital of the World in Plant City. It holds the record for the world's largest strawberry shortcake. It was made in 1999 and measured 827 square feet (77 sq m) and weighed 6,000 pounds (2,722 kg)!

SEE IT HERE!

THE DALÍ MUSEUM

This St. Petersburg museum houses the most comprehensive collection of the work of artist Salvador Dalí. Dalí was a leader of surrealism—an artistic movement of the 20th century. Surrealists often create imaginative, playful, and dreamlike artworks. Dalí's paintings, for example, include elephants with legs like stilts, melting clocks, and a floating rose. The Dalí Museum features his works and those of other surrealists. Visit their Web site for online activities, youth programs, and to learn more about Dalí: www.salvadordalimuseum.org

St. Petersburg

★ **Museum of Fine Arts:** Known for its collection of French Impressionist paintings, this museum has works by great artists including Monet, Gauguin, Renoir, Morisot, and O'Keeffe.

★ **Florida International Museum:** The Florida International Museum always has exciting exhibits on display, for example "Wolf to Woof: The Story of Dogs" and "Age of Armor," focusing on the world of medieval and Renaissance knights.

Sarasota

★ **John and Mable Ringling Museum of Art:** The official State Art Museum of Florida, this site also includes The Circus Museums, containing memorabilia from the Big Top, including parade wagons, photographs, and costumes!

CENTRAL

THINGS TO DO: Experience a magical kingdom, visit horse country, and take a cruise in a glass-bottom boat.

Orlando

★ **Walt Disney World Resort:** Meet Mickey at the Magic Kingdom, lift off at the Epcot Center, go wild at the Animal Kingdom, or plummet down the Tower of Terror at Disney-MGM Studios. With four theme parks and more than 40 attractions, you'll never want to leave!

★ **Universal Studios Orlando:** Relive some of your favorite movies and television shows, from *Shrek* to *Jimmy Neutron*. Enjoy themed thrill rides and become part of the action at Universal Studios!

★ **Gatorland:** Unleash your wild side at Orlando's only theme park with bite and attitude. Get up close and personal with gators and crocs, birds and bears, turtles and iguanas, and much more at the "Alligator Capital of the World."

Ocala

★ **Florida Horse Park:** Situated on 500 acres (200 ha) in the heart of Central Florida, this year-round, world-class facility hosts competitions, festivals, a polo club, and other great ways to horse around. Riders can enjoy hundreds of miles of pristine trails that wind through the lush Florida greenway.

Silver Springs

★ **Silver Springs Boat Tours:** Cruise in a glass-bottom boat along the crystal clear waters of the Silver River. Explore jungles of centuries-old cypress and nature's most spectacular animals. There are live concerts at the beautiful Twin Oaks Mansion and special events all year.

Silver Springs

Winter Park

★ **The Charles Hosmer Morse Museum of American Art:** This museum houses the world's best collection of the works of Louis Comfort Tiffany, famous for his beautiful jewelry, pottery, paintings, art glass, leaded-glass windows, and lamps. In addition, the museum exhibits other American art pottery, paintings, graphics, and decorative arts.

EAST CENTRAL

THINGS TO DO: Explore great photography, test your need for speed, and learn all about space travel.

Daytona Beach

★ **Daytona USA:** Rev up at Daytona USA, the official attraction of NASCAR at Daytona International Speedway, and home to the annual Daytona 500 race.

★ **Southeast Museum of Photography:** This museum has a renowned collection of historical and contemporary photography. You'll find examples of photojournalism, fine art, portraiture, landscape, commercial, and documentary photography.

★ **Museum of Arts and Sciences:** Spend a few hours at the premier arts and sciences museum of central Florida. On view are both traveling and permanent exhibitions, which include Coca-Cola memorabilia, railroad cars, teddy bears and race cars!

★ **Halifax Historical Museum:** Housed in the former 1910 Merchant's Bank building, the museum covers the history of the greater Daytona Beach area from 5,000 BCE to today. On display are artifacts relating to the Spanish and British colonial periods, pioneer families, World Wars I and II, and vintage Americana.

Ponce Inlet

★ **Ponce de Leon Inlet Lighthouse:** As a National Historic Landmark and one of the few surviving complete lighthouse stations in the country, this lighthouse is a treasure. Ready for a challenge? Climb its 203 steps to the top of the tower for a spectacular view of the Atlantic, inlet, and inland waters!

Cape Canaveral

★ **Kennedy Space Center:** For an out-of-this-world experience, take a tour of the launching pad for all of NASA's space flights and missions into outer space, and learn about the history of the missions themselves!

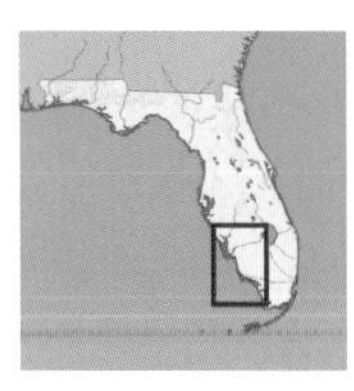

SOUTHWEST

THINGS TO DO: Learn about the history of the southwestern region of Florida, see the summer homes of the famous innovators Thomas Edison and Henry Ford, and watch out for crocodiles at the amazing Everglades!

SEE IT HERE!

SANIBEL ISLAND

If you want to see more seashells than anywhere else in the world, take a trip to Sanibel Island on the Gulf Coast. It is the Shell Capital of the whole western hemisphere. You'll be knee-deep in shells on the beaches of this lush island. Be sure to bring a bucket!

Fort Myers

★ **Southwest Florida Museum of History:** Meet Florida's early inhabitants—Seminole Indians, Spanish explorers, even giant ground sloths!

★ **Edison and Ford Winter Estates:** The Edison and Ford Winter Estates include the winter homes of the Edison and Ford families, tropical gardens, a laboratory, and a museum full of inventions, including 200 Edison phonographs.

Everglade City

★ **Everglades National Park:** This is the largest subtropical wilderness in the United States. The area boasts rare and endangered species, such as the American crocodile, Florida panther, and West Indian manatee! Learn more about these creatures as you tour this fragile ecosystem.

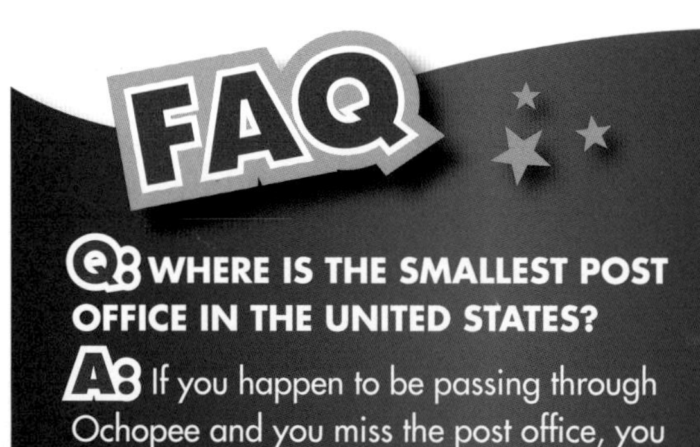

Q: WHERE IS THE SMALLEST POST OFFICE IN THE UNITED STATES?

A: If you happen to be passing through Ochopee and you miss the post office, you aren't alone. This city is the home of the smallest post office in the United States. It is 7 feet by 8 feet (2.1 m by 2.4 m), roughly the size of a coat closet, and was once an irrigation pipe shed for a tomato farm. Is there room in this post office for a bathroom? No. The closest one is about 1 mile (1.6 km) down the road.

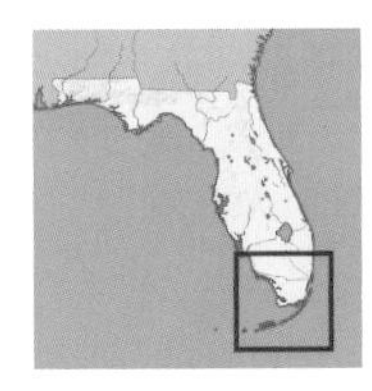

SOUTHEAST

THINGS TO DO: Enjoy Miami's famous art deco architecture and fabulous shops, play Frisbee on the beach, or get a look at local aquatic life!

Miami

★ **Miami Metrozoo:** Step inside this cageless zoo, which is five times larger than the average U.S. zoo, with 300 acres (121 ha), showcasing more than 2,000 animals representing almost 400 species!

★ **Miami Seaquarium:** Miami Seaquarium offers world-class marine life shows and attractions. Frolic with the comic genius of Salty and his laughable band of sea lions and discover the serene beauty of the endangered Florida manatee.

★ **Miami Beach:** Spend a relaxing day at Miami Beach, where you can swim, parasail, play volleyball, or read a good book under a beach umbrella!

Fort Lauderdale

★ **Dolphin World:** Swim with the dolphins in this interactive, high-energy learning experience that you won't soon forget.

Key Largo

★ **John Pennekamp State Park:** You can snorkel and scuba dive at the first underwater preserve in the nation! It is home to more than 600 species of colorful tropical fish and 40 brilliant types of coral.

Key West

★ **Ernest Hemingway Home and Museum:** Ernest Hemingway penned many of his best-known works while a resident of this tranquil environment. Take a guided tour of his estate, or stroll through the tropical gardens where "Papa" Hemingway once walked.

★ **Mallory Square Festival Marketplace:** Located at the center of the historic Key West waterfront, Mallory Square is filled with great shopping, fabulous restaurants, and the world-famous sunset celebration.

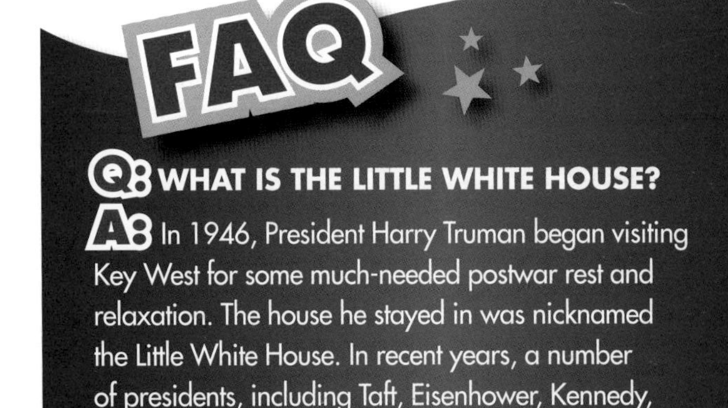

Q: WHAT IS THE LITTLE WHITE HOUSE?

A: In 1946, President Harry Truman began visiting Key West for some much-needed postwar rest and relaxation. The house he stayed in was nicknamed the Little White House. In recent years, a number of presidents, including Taft, Eisenhower, Kennedy, Carter, and Clinton, have stayed or held events there.

SCIENCE, TECHNOLOGY, & MATH PROJECTS

120

Make weather maps, graph population statistics, and research endangered species that live in the state.

PRIMARY VS. SECONDARY SOURCES

121

So what are primary and secondary sources and what's the diff? This section explains all that and where you can find them.

BIOGRAPHICAL DICTIONARY

133

This at-a-glance guide highlights some of the state's most important and influential people. Visit this section and read about their contributions to the state, the country, and the world.

RESOURCES

Books, Web sites, DVDs, and more. Take a look at these additional sources for information about the state.

137

WRITING PROJECTS

★ ★ ★

Compare and Contrast: When, Why, and How Did They Come?

Compare the migrations and explorations of the first Native people and the first European explorers to Florida! You can compare and contrast the following:

1. When their migrations began
2. How they traveled
3. Why they migrated
4. Where their journeys began and ended
5. What they found when they arrived

SEE: Chapters Two and Three, pages 29–35 and 37–47.

Create an Election Brochure or Web site!

Run for office!

Throughout this book, you've read about some of the issues that concern Florida today. As a candidate for governor of Florida, create a campaign brochure or Web site. Explain how you meet the qualifications to be governor of Florida; talk about the three or four major issues you'll focus on if you're elected. Remember, you'll be responsible for Florida's budget. How would you spend the taxpayers' money?

SEE: Chapter Seven, pages 85–93.

GO TO: Florida's Government Web site at www.myflorida.gov

Be a reporter or a talk-show host!

★ Choose one of the accomplished or interesting Floridians you've read about in this book as your interview subject.

★ Do your homework! Research that person so you know what questions to ask. You can go to Web sites mentioned in this book, or you can visit your library for a biography on the person.

★ Write out your questions. What do you think people would like to know about this person? Then, based on your research, provide the answers you think your subject would give.

SEE: Chapter Six, pages 69–83.

GO TO: The Florida Historical Society Web site at www.florida-historical-soc.org to find out more about famous public figures from Florida and their contributions.

ART PROJECTS

★ ★ ★

Create a PowerPoint Presentation or Visitors' Guide

Welcome to Florida!

Florida's a great place to visit, and to live! From its natural beauty to its bustling cities and historic sites, there's plenty to see and do. In your PowerPoint presentation or brochure, highlight 10 to 15 of Florida's amazing landmarks. Be sure to include:

★ a map of the state showing where these sites are located

★ photos, illustrations, Web links, natural history facts, geographic stats, climate and weather, plants and wildlife, recent discoveries

SEE: Chapter Nine, pages 105–115.

GO TO: The official Web site of Florida tourism at www.visitflorida.com. Download and print maps, photos, national landmark images, and vacation ideas for tourists.

Illustrate the Lyrics to the Florida State Song ("The Swanee River")

Use markers, paints, photos, collages, colored pencils, or computer graphics to illustrate the lyrics to the state song! Turn your illustrations into a picture book, or scan them into PowerPoint and add music!

SEE: The lyrics to "The Swanee River" on page 128.

GO TO: The Florida state Web site at www.myflorida.gov to find out more about the origin of the Florida state song.

State Quarter Project

From 1999 to 2008, the U.S. Mint introduced new quarters commemorating each of the 50 states in the order that they were admitted to the Union. Each state's quarter features a unique design on its back, or reverse.

★ Go to www.usmint.gov/kids and find out what's featured on the back of the Florida quarter.

★ Research the significance of each image. Who designed the quarter? Who chose the final design?

★ Design your own Florida quarter. What images would you choose for the reverse?

★ Make a poster showing the Florida quarter and label each image.

SCIENCE, TECHNOLOGY, & MATH PROJECTS

★ ★ ★

Graph Population Statistics!

★ Compare population statistics (such as ethnic background, birth, death, and literacy rates) in Florida counties or major cities.

★ In your graph or chart, look at population density. Explain what the population statistics show, graph one set of population statistics, and write a paragraph explaining what the graphs reveal.

SEE: Chapter Six, pages 70–73.

GO TO: The official Web site for the U.S. Census Bureau at www.census.gov, and http://quickfacts.census.gov/qfd/states/12000.html, to find out more about population statistics, how they work, and what the statistics are for Florida.

Create a Weather Map of Florida!

Use your knowledge of Florida's geography to research and identify conditions that result in specific weather events, including thunderstorms and hurricanes. What is it about the geography of Florida that makes it vulnerable to hurricanes? Create a weather map or poster that shows the weather patterns over the state. To accompany your map, explain the technology used to measure weather phenomena such as hurricanes and provide data.

SEE: Chapter One, pages 9–20.

GO TO: The National Oceanic and Atmospheric Administration's National Weather Service Web site at www.weather.gov for weather maps and forecasts for Florida.

Track Endangered Species

Using your knowledge of Florida's wildlife, research what animals and plants are endangered or threatened.

★ Find out what the state is doing to protect these species.

★ Chart known populations of the animals and plants, and report on changes in certain geographical areas.

SEE: Chapter One, pages 24–27.

GO TO: The U.S. Fish and Wildlife site at www.fws.gov/endangered/or other Florida-specific sites such as www.endangeredspecie.com/states/fl.htm

PRIMARY VS. SECONDARY SOURCES

★ ★ ★

What's the Diff?

Your teacher may require at least one or two primary sources and one or two secondary sources for your assignment. So, what's the difference between the two?

- **Primary sources are original.** You are reading the actual words of someone's diary, journal, letter, autobiography or interview. Primary sources can also be photographs, maps, prints, cartoons, news/film footage, posters, first-person newspaper articles, drawings, musical scores, and recordings. By the way, when you conduct a survey, interview someone, shoot a video, or take photographs to include in a project—you are creating primary sources!
- **Secondary sources are what you find in encyclopedias, textbooks, articles, biographies, and almanacs.** These are written by a person or group of people who tell about something that happened to someone else. Secondary sources also recount what another person said or did. This book is an example of a secondary source.

Now that you know what primary sources are—where can you find them?

- **Your school or local library:** Check the library catalog for collections of original writings, government documents, musical scores, and so on. Some of this material may be stored on microfilm. The Library of Congress Web site (www.loc.gov) is an excellent online resource for primary source materials.
- **Historical societies:** These organizations keep historical documents, photographs, and other materials. Staff members can help you find what you are looking for. History museums are also great places to see primary sources first-hand.
- **The Internet:** There are lots of sites that have primary sources you can download and use in a project or assignment.

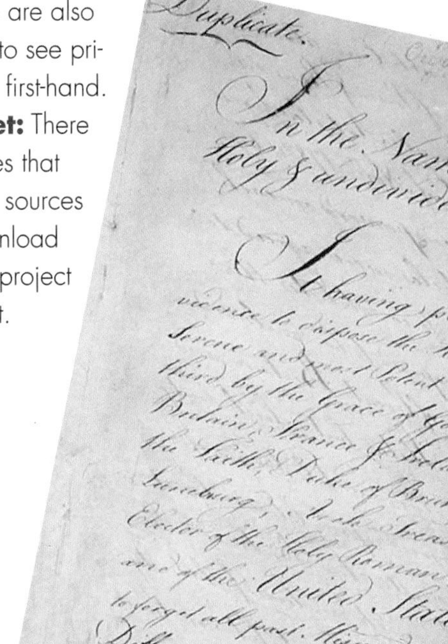

Duplicate.

In the Name

Holy & undivided

TIMELINE

U.S. Events | **1500** | **Florida Events**

1513
Juan Ponce de León lands on the shores of Florida.

1528
Pánfilo de Narváez lands at Tampa Bay with 400 men.

1539
Hernando de Soto comes to Florida with ships and 600 people.

1564
The Huguenots arrive from France and build a settlement.

1565 (U.S. Events)
Spanish admiral Pedro Menéndez de Avilés founds St. Augustine, Florida, the oldest continuously occupied European settlement in the continental United States.

1565 (Florida Events)
King Philip II sends Pedro Menéndez de Avilés to Florida.

1600

1607 (U.S. Events)
The first permanent English settlement is established in North America at Jamestown.

1700

1763
The Treaty of Paris gives Florida to Britain in exchange for Cuba.

1770s
Creek Indians and others become known as the Seminole.

1776 (U.S. Events)
Thirteen American colonies declare their independence from Britain, marking the beginning of the Revolutionary War.

1781
Spain captures West Florida and then East Florida.

U.S. Events	1800	Florida Events
		1817 The First Seminole War begins.
		1819 Spain gives up its claim on Florida.
1830 The Indian Removal Act forces eastern Native American groups to relocate west of the Mississippi River.		**1830** The Indian Removal Act is passed by Congress.
		1835 The Second Seminole War begins.
		1837 Osceola is taken prisoner.
		1845 Florida becomes a state.
1846–48 The United States fights a war with Mexico over western territories in the Mexican War.		
		1855 The Third Seminole War begins.
	1900	
1917–18 The United States is involved in World War I.		
		1926 The Great Miami Hurricane hits Florida.
		1928 Okeechobee Hurricane hits Florida.
1929 The stock market crashes, plunging the United States into the Great Depression.		
		1960s Waves of Cuban immigrants begin coming to Florida.
		1963 NASA names the John F. Kennedy Space Center.
1964–73 The United States engages in the Vietnam War.		**1964** Dr. Martin Luther King Jr. visits Florida.

U.S. Events

Florida Events

1969
Apollo 11 lands on the moon.

1971
Walt Disney World opens.

1977
Capitol building is built in Tallahassee.

1982
EPCOT opens.

1987
Bob Martinez becomes the first Latino governor of the state.

1991 (U.S.)
The United States and other nations engage in the brief Persian Gulf War against Iraq.

1992
Hurricane Andrew hits.

2000

2000
The controversial presidential election focuses on Florida voting practices.

2001 (U.S.)
Terrorists hijack four U.S. aircraft and crash them into the World Trade Center in New York City, the Pentagon in Washington, DC., and a Pennsylvania field, killing thousands.

2003 (U.S.)
The United States and coalition forces invade Iraq.

2004
Four hurricanes make landfall in Florida.

2005
Hurricane Wilma hits and leaves 3,200,000 without power.

GLOSSARY

animatronics puppets or other figures that are designed in an electronic way

bigoted having unfair opinions of a group, based on that group's religion, race, or other factors

boycott the organized refusal to use a service or buy a product, as a form of protest

colonize to establish a colony, which is a new settlement with ties to another governing state

concentrate a food that has excess water removed from it

ecosystem organisms and their environment

guerrilla describing soldiers who don't belong to regular armies; they often use surprise attacks and other uncommon battle tactics

ice age a period in history when large parts of Earth were covered in ice; there have been four such periods; the most recent ended 10,000 years ago

infection the reproduction of microorganisms within the body, creating illness

integration the incorporation of all races and groups into society; the opposite of segregation

International Biosphere Reserve a protected sample of the world's major ecosystem types

jetties structures that extend into bodies of water to affect the current or protect harbors

keys low islands or reefs; the word *key* comes from the the Spanish word *cayo*, which means "little island"

oases places that provide shelter or relief; the singular is *oasis*

paleo ancient, prehistoric

peninsula a large mass of land that extends into a body of water

polyps nonmoving marine creatures that attach to rocks and coral

resin clear or light-colored material that is secreted by trees and other plants; used in varnishes, printing inks, and other products

segregated separated from others, based on race, class, ethnic group, or other factors

sinkholes natural depressions in the ground formed by soil, sediment, or rock as underlying rocks are dissolved by groundwater

stalactites columns or pillars formed on the roof of a cave from dripping groundwater

stalagmites columns or pillars formed on the floor of a cave from dripping groundwater

FAST FACTS

State Symbols

Statehood date March 3, 1845, the 27th state
Origin of state name Named by Ponce de León on Easter Sunday, 1513
State capital Tallahassee
State nickname Sunshine State
State motto "In God we trust"
State animal Florida panther
State beverage Orange juice
State freshwater fish Florida largemouth bass
State saltwater fish Atlantic sailfish
State bird Mockingbird
State flower Orange blossom
State gem Moonstone
State stone Agatized coral
State song "Swanee River" See page 128.
State tree Sabal palmetto palm
State fair Tampa (early to mid-February)

State flag

State seal

Geography

Total area; rank 65,755 square miles (170,305 sq km); 22nd
Land; rank 53,927 square miles (139,671 sq km); 26th
Water; rank 11,828 square miles (30,634 sq km); 3rd
Inland water; rank 4,672 square miles (12,100 sq km); 4th
Coastal water; rank 1,311 square miles (3,395 sq km); 6th
Territorial water; rank 5,845 square miles (15,139 sq km); 2nd
Geographic center In Hernando County, 12 miles (19 km) northwest of Brooksville
Latitude 24° 30′ N to 31° N
Longitude 79° 48′ W to 87° 38′ W
Highest point In Walton County, 345 feet (105 m)
Lowest point Sea level along Atlantic Ocean
Largest city Jacksonville
Number of counties 67
Longest river St. Johns River, 275 miles (443 km)

Population

Population; rank (2006 estimate) 18,089,888; 4th
Density (2006 estimate) 335 persons per square mile (130 per sq km)
Population distribution 89% urban, 11% rural
Race (as of 2005) White persons: 80.4%
Black persons: 15.7%*
Asian persons: 2.1%*
American Indian and Alaska Native persons: 0.4%*
Native Hawaiian and Other Pacific Islanders: 0.1%*
Persons reporting two or more races: 1.2%
Persons of Hispanic or Latino origin: 19.5%†
White persons not Hispanic: 62.1%

** Includes persons reporting only one race.*
† Hispanics may be of any race, so they are also included in applicable race categories.

Weather

Record high temperature 109°F (44°C) at Monticello on June 29, 1931
Record low temperature –2°F (–19°C) at Tallahassee on February 13, 1899
Average July temperature, Jacksonville 82°F (28°C)
Average January temperature, Jacksonville 53°F (12°C)
Average yearly precipitation, Jacksonville 52.3 inches (132.8 cm)
Average July temperature, Miami 84°F (29°C)
Average January temperature, Miami 69°F (21°C)
Average yearly precipitation, Miami 58.5 inches (148.6 cm)

STATE SONG

"The Swanee River"

by Stephen C. Foster

Stephen C. Foster, one of America's best-loved musical storytellers, wrote "The Swanee River (Old Folks at Home)" in 1851. The Suwannee River flows in a southern direction from the Okeefenokee Swamp in Georgia to the Gulf of Mexico in Florida, slicing the Florida Panhandle from the rest of the state. Foster is reported to have chosen the spelling "Swanee" because this two-syllable version fit nicely into the music he had composed.

In 1935, "The Swanee River" became the official state song, replacing "Florida, My Florida," which had been adopted as the state song in 1913.

Way down upon the Swanee River,
Far, far away,
There's where my heart is turning ever,
There's where the old folks stay.
All up and down the whole creation,
Sadly I roam,
Still longing for the old plantation,
And for the old folks at home.

(Chorus)
All the world is sad and dreary
Everywhere I roam.
O brothers, how my heart grows weary,
Far from the old folks at home.

All 'round the little farm I wander'd,
When I was young;
Then many happy days I squander'd,
Many the songs I sung.
When I was playing with my brother,
Happy was I.
Oh, take me to my kind old mother,
There let me live and die.

One little hut among the bushes,
One that I love.
Still sadly to my memory rushes,
No matter where I rove.
When will I see the bees a humming,
All 'round the comb?
When shall I hear the banjo strumming,
Down in my good old home.

NATURAL AREAS AND HISTORIC SITES

National Parks

Three national parks are in Florida, including *Everglades National Park*, a vast wilderness covering the southern tip of the Florida peninsula, and *Dry Tortugas National Park*, a collection of seven islands and their surrounding waters about 65 miles (105 km) west of Key West.

National Preserves

The state has two national preserves, including *Big Cypress National Preserve*, which adjoins the Everglades.

National Seashores

Florida is home to two national seashores, including *Canaveral National Seashore*, which is a preserved area north of Kennedy Space Center.

National Monuments

Two national monuments are in Florida: *Fort Matanzas*, and *Castillo de San Marcos National Monument* (St. Augustine), which is the oldest masonry fort in the United States.

National Memorials

Florida is home to two national memorials: *De Soto National Memorial* (Tampa), which commemorates Hernando de Soto and his landing in Florida in 1539, and *Fort Caroline National Memorial* (Jacksonville), which is near the site of the second French fort in the United States.

National Forests

Three national forests are in the state, including *Apalachicola National Forest*, which is in the Florida Panhandle and contains beautiful swamps, rivers, and lakes, and *Ocala National Forest*, a huge wilderness area of pines and swamps.

State Parks and Forests

Florida has 159 state parks. They include *John Pennekamp Coral Reef State Park* (95 percent of which is underwater) and *Myakka River State Park* (the largest state park in Florida). Florida's state forests cover nearly 1,000,000 acres (404,685 ha).

SPORTS TEAMS

NCAA Teams (Division I)

Bethune-Cookman College *Wildcats*
Florida A&M University *Rattlers*
Florida Atlantic University *Owls*
Florida International University *Golden Panthers*
Florida State *Seminoles*
Jacksonville University *Dolphins*
North Florida University *Ospreys*
Stetson University *Hatters*
University of Central Florida *Knights*
University of Florida *Gators*
University of Miami *Hurricanes*
University of South Florida *Bulls*

PROFESSIONAL SPORTS TEAMS

Major League Baseball

Florida Marlins
Tampa Bay Devil Rays

National Basketball Association

Miami Heat
Orlando Magic

National Football League

Miami Dolphins
Tampa Bay Buccaneers
Jacksonville Jaguars

National Hockey League

Florida Panthers
Tampa Bay Lightning

CULTURAL INSTITUTIONS

Libraries

The St. Augustine Free Public Library is the oldest library in Florida. It opened as a subscription library in 1874. Library members gave money to buy books, which they could use without charge. The state's first free, tax-supported library opened in Jacksonville in 1905. Today, Florida has about 120 public libraries, many of which are county or regional library systems with several branches.

Museums

The John and Mable Ringling Museum of Art in Sarasota is noted for its baroque art collection. Also on the grounds are the Ringling mansion and the museum's Circus Galleries.

The Cummer Gallery of Art in Jacksonville is well known for its collections of significant European and American paintings and for its world-renowned collection of early Meissen porcelain.

The Norton Gallery and School of Art in West Palm Beach is internationally known for its distinguished permanent collection featuring 19th- and 20th-century European and American art, Chinese art, contemporary art, and photography.

Miami Metrozoo is a large zoo that displays animals in settings modeled after different parts of the world. It also features a monorail and an aviary where exotic birds fly freely.

Stephen Foster Folk Culture Center State Park, in north-central Florida, offers tours of the Stephen Foster Museum and Carillon Tower, the opportunity to see working artists in Craft Square, and canoe and kayak rides on the Suwannee River.

Performing Arts

Florida has two major dance companies, one major professional theater, seven major symphony orchestras, and five major opera companies.

Universities and Colleges

In 2006, Florida had 179 colleges and universities, and 41 were public.

ANNUAL EVENTS

January–March

Orange Bowl Football Game in Miami area (January)

Greek Epiphany Ceremony in Tarpon Springs (January)

Zora Neale Hurston Festival of the Arts and Humanities in Eatonville (January)

Old Island Days in Key West (January–March)

Black Hills Passion Play in Lake Wales (mid-February through Easter)

Daytona 500 Auto Race in Daytona Beach (February)

Edison Pageant of Light in Fort Myers (February)

Florida Citrus Festival in Winter Haven (February)

Florida State Fair in Tampa (February)

Swamp Buggy Days in Naples (February)

Festival of States in St. Petersburg (March–April)

Winter Park Sidewalk Art Festival in Winter Park (March)

Motorcycle Week in Daytona Beach (March)

Ringling Museum's Medieval Fair in Sarasota (March)

April–June

DeSoto Festival in Bradenton (April)

Easter Week Festival in St. Augustine (April)

Flying High Circus in Tallahassee (April)

Fiesta of Five Flags in Pensacola (May–June)

Florida Folk Festival in White Springs (May)

International Festival in Miami (May)

Pensacola Shark Rodeo in Pensacola (June)

"Cross and Sword" Official State Play in St. Augustine (June–July)

July–September

Rodeos in Arcadia and Kissimmee (Fourth of July weekend)

Pepsi 400 Auto Race in Daytona Beach (Fourth of July)

Days in Spain in St. Augustine (August)

October–December

Beaux Arts Promenade in Fort Lauderdale (November)

Pioneer Settlement for the Creative Arts Fall Jamboree in Barberville (November)

Gator Bowl Festival and Football Game in Jacksonville (December or January)

Blockbuster Bowl Football Game in Miami (December or January)

Florida Citrus Bowl Football Game in Orlando (last week in December or first week in January)

BIOGRAPHICAL DICTIONARY

Julian "Cannonball" Adderley (1928–1975) was a jazz alto saxophonist during the 1950s and 1960s. He was born in Tampa.

Wallace Amos Jr. See page 102.

Dave Barry (1947–) is a Pulitzer Prize–winning columnist who wrote for the *Miami Herald* for more than 20 years. He was born in New York.

"Banana George" Blair (1915–) is the world's oldest water-skier. He was born in Ohio and lives in Winter Haven.

Edward Bloor (1950–) is an author of books for young adults. He was born in New Jersey and lives in Winter Garden.

Edward Bok (1863–1930) was an editor and Pulitzer Prize–winning author. Born in The Netherlands, he created the "Singing Tower" in Lake Wales.

Pat Boone (1934–) is a singer, actor, and conservative commentator. He was born in Jacksonville.

Wayne Brady (1972–) is a comedian, singer, and television personality most known for *Whose Line Is It Anyway?* He was born in Orlando.

Fernando Bujones (1955–2005) was a well-known dancer and dance teacher. He was hailed as the greatest American male dancer of his generation. Born in Miami, he served for a time as the artistic director of the Orlando Ballet.

John Ellis "Jeb" Bush (1953–) served as governor of Florida from 1999 to 2007. Born in Texas, he is the son of President George H. W. Bush and the brother of President George W. Bush.

Steve "Lefty" Carlton (1944–) is one of the best pitchers to have ever played major league baseball. He was born in Miami.

Jacqueline Cochran (1906–1980) was a skilled pilot who set more speed and altitude records than any other pilots of the time, male or female. She was born in Muscogee.

Jacqueline Cochran

Dana A. Dorsey (1872–1940) was born in Georgia, but moved to Miami to work as a carpenter on the Florida East Coast Railroad. He went on to be a banker, businessman, and philanthropist and was Florida's first African American millionaire.

Wayne Brady

Tim Dorsey (1961–) is a writer of crime novels often set in Florida. He was born in Indiana, but grew up in Riviera Beach. He currently lives in Tampa.

Marjory Stoneman Douglas See page 17.

Gloria Estefan See page 81.

Chris Evert (1954–) is a champion tennis player who captured 18 Grand Slam titles. She was born in Fort Lauderdale.

Maurice Ferre (1935–) was elected mayor of Miami and served for a total of six terms (until 1985). He was the first Puerto Rican to be elected mayor of a major U.S. city.

Henry Flagler See page 57.

Jonathan Gibbs (1821–1874) was born in Philadelphia. He became a Presbyterian minister and traveled south after the Civil War to open churches. In 1867, he moved to Florida and was elected to Florida's constitutional convention. Then he served as Florida's secretary of state and superintendent of public instruction. He might be called the father of Florida public schools.

Maurice Ferre

Mary Grizzle (1921–2006) served in the Florida senate from 1978 to 1990 and was a pioneer in environmental and women's rights issues. She was a resident of Belleair Shore.

Chris Evert

Alfred Hair (1941–1970) was the leader of a group of artists known as the Highwaymen. They were famous for painting Florida landscapes.

Carl Hiaasen See page 80.

Zora Neale Hurston See page 79.

May Mann Jennings (1872–1963) fought for countless causes, including reservations for local Seminole Indians and making the highways more beautiful. She was the one behind the development of a state forestry department and spent more than 30 years fighting to preserve the Everglades.

James Weldon Johnson See page 55.

Betty Mae Tiger Jumper See page 64.

Jack Kerouac (1922–1969) was a novelist, writer, poet, and artist from the Beat Generation. Born in Massachusetts, he lived for many years in Orlando and St. Petersburg.

Ed Leedskalnin (1887–1951) was the creator of the Coral Castle in Homestead. He was born in Latvia.

Lue Gim Gong (1860–1925) was born in China, but settled with his wife in DeLand, Florida. Remarkably talented with plants, his claim to fame was an orange that was a cross between the "Harts Late" Valencia and the "Mediterranean Sweet." The Lue Gim Gong orange was both sweet and resistant to frost. It is still sold under the name Valencia.

Tino Martinez (1967–) was a first baseman in major league baseball. He played for the New York Yankees, Tampa Bay Devil Rays, Saint Louis Cardinals, and Seattle Mariners. He was born in Tampa.

Butterfly McQueen (1911–1995) was a film and television actor who made her debut in *Gone with the Wind*. She was born in Tampa.

Francisco Menendez See page 42.

Clarence Bloomfield Moore (1852–1936) was born in Philadelphia and spent most of his life investigating hundreds of Native American mounds in southern states, including Florida.

Henry T. Moore (1905–1951) was born in Houston, Florida, and was a noted civil rights activist. He and his wife, Harriette, were murdered by the Ku Klux Klan.

Jim Morrison (1943–1971) was a famous rock singer and leader of The Doors. He was born in Melbourne.

William Dunn Moseley See page 88.

Shaquille O'Neal (1972–) is one of the best-known professional basketball players. A dominant center, "Shaq" has played for the Orlando Magic, the Los Angeles Lakers, and the Miami Heat. He was born in New Jersey.

Osceola See page 88.

Tom Petty (1950–) is a rock 'n' roll musician and leader of The Heartbreakers. He was born in Gainesville.

Sidney Poitier (1927–) is an acclaimed actor and film director. He was born en route to Miami from the Bahamas.

Juan Ponce de León (c. 1460–1521) was a Spanish explorer who discovered Florida while searching for the fountain of youth.

A. Philip Randolph (1889–1979) was a labor leader and civil rights activist. He was born in Crescent City.

Marjorie Kinnan Rawlings (1896–1953) was the author of *The Yearling*. She was born in Washington, D.C., but spent many years living on an orange farm in Hawthorne.

Janet Reno (1938–) was raised in Miami and was the state attorney for what is now Miami-Dade County. During the Clinton Administration (1993–2001), she served as U.S. attorney general—the first woman to hold that position. She held that office longer than any other attorney general since 1961. In 2002, she ran for the Democratic nomination for governor of Florida, but lost.

Janet Reno

Burt Reynolds (1936–) is an actor who has made dozens of films. He grew up in West Palm Beach and went to Florida State University.

Charles Ringling (1864–1926) and **John Ringling (1866–1936)** are cofounders of the Ringling Brothers and Barnum and Bailey circus. Their winter headquarters was in Sarasota.

David Robinson See page 82.

Jennifer Rodriguez (1976–) is an Olympic speed skater. She was born in Miami and is the only Winter Olympian to hail from south Florida.

Ileana Ros-Lehtinen See page 93.

David Sanborn (1945–) is a jazz saxophonist. He was born in Tampa.

Wesley Snipes (1962–) is an actor, martial artist, and film producer. He was born in Orlando.

Jennifer Rodriguez

Joseph Warren Stilwell (1883–1946) was a four-star general in the U.S. Army. He was born in Palatka.

Rob Thomas

Rob Thomas (1962–) is a popular singer who used to be the lead for the Orlando-based band Matchbox Twenty. He was born in Germany, but raised in Florida.

Ben Vereen (1946–) is a Tony Award–winning actor, singer, and dancer. He was born in Miami.

Josiah T. Walls (1842–1905) was born as a slave in Virginia. After the Civil War, he settled in Alachua County. In 1871, he was elected as the sole representative from Florida to the U.S. Congress.

Vicente Martinez Ybor (1818–1896) was a cigar maker who moved from Cuba to Tampa. He built a factory there and named it Ybor City, which became the cigar capital of the world.

RESOURCES

BOOKS

Nonfiction

Eagan, Rachel. *Ponce de León: Exploring Florida and Puerto Rico.* New York: Crabtree Children's Books, 2005.
Englar, Mary. *The Seminole: The First People of Florida.* Mankato, Minn.: Capstone Press, 2006.
Heinrichs, Ann. *Florida.* Mankato, Minn.: Compass Point Books, 2006.
Lantz, Peggy, and Wendy Hale. *The Young Naturalist's Guide to Florida.* Sarasota: Pineapple Press, 2006.
Murray, Julie. *Florida.* New York: Buddy Books, 2005.
Weitzel, Kelley G. *Journeys with Florida's Indians.* Gainesville: University Press of Florida, 2002.
Woods, Michael. *Hurricanes.* Minneapolis: Lerner Publications, 2006.

Fiction

Baglio, Ben. *Into the Blue* (Dolphin Diaries). New York: Scholastic Paperbacks, 2002.
Bloor, Edward. *Tangerine.* New York: Harcourt Children's Books, 1997.
Douglas, Marjory Stoneman. *Alligator Crossing.* Minneapolis: Millweed Editions, 2003 reissue.
Hiaasen, Carl. *Hoot.* New York: Knopf Books for Young Readers, 2002.
Rawlings, Marjorie Kinnan. *The Yearling.* New York: Aladdin, 2001 reissue.
Shore, Liz. *The Key Keepers Mystery: The Game Begins.* Frederick, Md.: PublishAmerica, 2006.

DVDs

The Best of: Florida in 60 Minutes. International Video Projects, 2004.
Destination: Florida's Gulf Coast. Discovery Channel, 2006.
Everglades: Florida's River of Grass. Pro-Active Entertainment, 2007.
Florida Springs: The Unexplored Florida. Matrox Films, 2004.
The Highwaymen: Florida's Outsider Artists. Janson Media, 2003.
Travel Florida: State and National Parks. International Video Projects, 2004.
Water's Journey: The Hidden Rivers of Florida. Karst Productions, 2003.

WEB SITES AND ORGANIZATIONS

A Brief History of Florida
www.flheritage.com/facts/history/summary/
For more information about the state's history.

Everglades National Park
www.nps.gov/ever/
To get details about this amazing natural area.

Florida Heritage Collection
http://palmm.fcla.edu/fh/
For more information about the state's history and ongoing projects.

Museum of Science and Industry
www.mosi.org
For details about the latest exhibits, films, and events.

Old City
www.oldcity.com
To learn more about St. Augustine, the nation's oldest city.

Online Sunshine
www.leg.state.fl.us/Welcome/index.cfm?CFID=8390896&CFTOKEN=84187973
To learn more about Florida's government.

Salvador Dalí Museum
www.salvadordalimuseum.org/home.html
To take an online tour of this art collection.

Visit Florida
www.visitflorida.com/
For help in planning your next vacation.

Vizcaya Museum and Gardens
www.vizcayamuseum.org/
To learn more about this museum in Miami-Dade County.

INDEX

★ ★ ★

AUTHOR'S TIPS AND SOURCE NOTES

★ ★ ★

Researching this state was great fun because I personally have fabulous memories of Florida. I never lived there, but each spring break, my family and I would head off to the sun and surf to get as far away from the Indiana cold as possible.

It was during my research that I came across a book I wished I'd had back when I was a kid. Called *The Young Naturalist's Guide to Florida* by Peggy Lantz and Wendy Hale (Pineapple Press, 2006), it shows families different ways to help protect Florida's natural treasures. I also found a novel based on Florida's geography called *The Key Keepers Mystery: The Game Begins* by Liz Shore (PublishAmerica, 2006). It had kids chasing clues throughout St. Augustine, the Everglades, and into the islands of the Keys. Another source that helped me appreciate Florida's beauty was a DVD called *The Best of: Florida in 60 Minutes* (International Video Projects, 2004). I especially liked another DVD named *The Highwaymen: Florida's Outsider Artists* (Janson Media, 2003).

Writing this book, I learned a great deal more about Florida. It made me want to pack up my sandals and sunscreen again and head south to check out all I read about.

Photographs © 2008: age fotostock: 98 (Robert W. Ginn), 76 (Jeff Greenberg); Alamy Images: cover (Rob Crandall), 97 top (David R. Frazier Photolibrary, Inc.), 96, 97 left (Melvyn Longhurst), 110 bottom right (M Stock), 112 (Dennis MacDonald), 46 (North Wind Picture Archives), 75 top (M. Timothy O'Keefe), 107 bottom (Purcell Team); Animals Animals: 8, 9 left (Werner Layer), 26 top (Lynn Stone), 28 main, 29 left (Fred Whitehead); AP Images: 135 (Dennis Cook), 134 bottom (Tony Gutierrez), 83 (Mark Humphrey), 78 (Robert E. Klein), 113 bottom, 132 (John Raoux), 17 right (Lynne Sladky), 58 bottom, 133 top; Art Resource, NY/Bildarchiv Preussischer Kulturbesitz: 4 center right, 29 top, 29 bottom, 34; Aurora Photos/Robb Kendrick: 82; Buddy Mays/Travel Stock: 17 left; Corbis Images: 102 (Andy Warhol Foundation), 68, 69 left (Tony Arruza), 38, 57 inset (Bettmann), 100 (William Boyce), 13 (Kevin Fleming), 5 bottom left, 106 right, 114 bottom (Dave G. Houser), 19 (Bob Krist), 119 left (Lake County Museum), 22 (Owaki-Kulla), 136 bottom (Christina Pahnke/ NewSport), 88 top (Hilda Perez), 5 top right, 59 top, 65, 123 (Roger Ressmeyer), 93 (Reuters), 74 top, 127 (Tony Savino/Sygma), 54, 79 top; Courtesy of Florida Department of State: 64, 88 bottom (The Florida Memory Project), 95, 126 left; Courtesy of Sally Corporation: 103; Dembinsky Photo Assoc.: 15 (Susan Blanchet), 10 (NASA); Florida International Museum: 111 bottom left; Getty Images: 59 bottom (Terry Ashe/Time & Life Pictures), 111 bottom right, 133 bottom (Frederick M. Brown), 58 top, 59 left (FPG), 60 (R. B. Holt), 79 bottom (George Karger), 62 (Robert W. Kelley/ Time & Life Pictures), 18 (Dave King), 4 bottom left, 69 top right, 75 bottom (Jeremy Liebman), 61 (MPI), 85 top, 94, 126 (Thomas Northcut), 26 bottom (Mike Parry), 55 (Charles H. Phillips/Time & Life Pictures); iStockphoto: 116 bottom, 130 bottom (Geoffrey Black), 130 top (David Freund), 128 (Vladislav Lebedinski), 49 bottom; Landov, LLC: 80 top (Andrew Harrer/Bloomberg News), 134 top (Don Morley/PA Photos); Masterfile/Bill Brooks: 109; NASA: cover inset; National Archives and Records Administration: 37 bottom left, 121; Nativestock.com/Marilyn "Angel" Wynn: 28 bottom right, 35, 47; NEWSCOM/Charles Trainor Jr.: 77; North Wind Picture Archives: back cover, 5 top left, 36 bottom, 39, 44, 48 top, 48 bottom, 49 left, 50, 51, 122; Photo Researchers, NY: 37 bottom right (Guy Gillette), 110 top left (Jeffrey Greenberg), 5 bottom right, 110 top right (Michael Patrick O'Neill), 9 right, 14, 16, 108 bottom (Millard H. Sharp); PhotoEdit: 70 (Jeff Greenberg), 73 (Dennis McDonald), 86, 124 (Mary Steinbacher); Retna Ltd./Francine Daveta: 136 top; Reuters: 92; ShutterStock, Inc.: 41 top (Jubal Harshaw), 4 center left, 25 (Kovalev Serguei); Superstock, Inc.: 33 (A.K.G. Berlin), 36 top, 37 top left (Cummer Museum of Art & Gardens, Jacksonville, FL), 84, 85 left (Richard Cummins), 4 top, 28 bottom left (Museum of Natural Antiquities), 30, 49 top, 52; The Art Archive/Picture Desk: 80 bottom (Mirisch/United Artists/The Kobal Collection), 37 top right, 41 bottom (Alfredo Dagli Orti); The Granger Collection, New York: 43, 45, 57 main, 118; The Image Works: 66, 74 bottom (Jeff Greenberg), 42 (Mary Evans Picture Library), 21 (Jim Sulley/Newscast), 81 (UPPA/Topham), 31 left, 31 right (Werner Forman Archive/University Museum, Philadelphia); Tom Stack & Associates, Inc.: 24; US Mint: 116 top, 119 right; Visuals Unlimited/Albert Copley: 11.

Maps by Map Hero, Inc.

WITHDRAWN